Th
Homes(

Part 1
Starting Out:
Help, Support And Encouragement

By

Sonya Chappell

Dedication

To my husband Rob for making homeschooling the best decision we've ever made.

To Julie Gilbert, my friend from homeschooling-ideas.com, who has taught me so much. She is my inspiration and guide. Thank you for designing such brilliant book covers for me.

To all my Facebook fans and members of the Courageous Homeschooling Facebook Group. Thank you for proving that homeschooling works so much better when we come together to support each other.

To Sylvia Kerslake and Joe Dugdale from www.sylv.net who offer a great service for self-publishing authors. Thank you so much for your help – so kind of you.

And finally to my Mom, who homeschooled me all those years ago. Love you Mom!

Contents

Introduction

Homeschooling encouragement........... 15

A glimpse into our days...............25

Starting Out

Top tips for new homeschoolers......... 37

Why do people choose to homeschool?...........43

Can I cope?....................51

I feel so overwhelmed.................57

Too many subjects to teach................63

Will my child miss out by not going to school?....71

Being judged by others..................77

I'm not good enough to teach my child............ 83

What if I fail my child?.......................89

Homeschooling fears..........................95

Am I doing enough? Am I doing it right?...........99

How do I tell my partner?.....................103

Will I damage my relationship with my children? 109

How do I deal with nosy neighbors?.................. 113

What if my children won't do any school work?.. 123

Socialization: What about friends?................ 127

Other people's anxt. over socialization............... 133

Conclusion

Things I am grateful for......................... 139

An inspirational homeschool Mom's story........... 143

More help........................ 147

Introduction

Starting homeschooling is often the scariest decision you will ever make!

It's a time when you feel at your most vulnerable – both because you worry you aren't good enough to do it and more importantly because you don't want to mess up your child's future.

The Courageous Homeschooling Handbook will show you that we all share these fears but together we can support each other through them. You will discover that teaching your child at home is the **most fulfilling thing** you have ever done.

I am one of the few second generation homeschoolers taught at home myself, and my homeschool son is now at **Oxford University**. I run a successful website at *www.homeschool-activities.com* with 10,000+ Facebook fans.

I set up a **Courageous Homeschooling Facebook support group** which offers friendship and encouragement and where no one judges anyone else. We share resources and run a coffee club so we can all meet up for a virtual drink.

The Courageous Homeschooling Handbook brings together the **collective wisdom** of this fabulous group of women (and some gents!) from all over the world who know exactly what it feels like.

They have been brave enough to share their worries and concerns, and then offer their own take on how they have overcome the hurdles we all face.

You will find in this Handbook genuine cries from the heart, and you will be **uplifted** by seeing how together we can all help each other gain perspective and strength.

This is the first part of three Courageous Homeschooling Handbooks which together provide a complete guide to carry you right through your homeschooling journey.

The advice you will find is all the richer because it comes from such a variety of perspectives and experiences based on the firm conviction that we are all here to support each other **however we choose to homeschool** because we each know our own child best.

This Handbook covers the beginning of homeschooling when you first contemplate taking the plunge.   It is broken into sections based on the most common and difficult questions that have come up in the Courageous group.

"I think we all get wobbly moments from time to time. There are so many things in life that can make

*us feel under pressure or doubting ourselves. That's why the Courageous Homeschooling group is so **helpful** as the amazing parents here share different ideas and perspectives, and **caring support**, and it puts us back on track." ~ Brigid*

You will see everything from worries about whether you can cope, how to deal with being judged by others and the perennial concern over whether your child will make friends. You'll find a section of top tips for new homeschoolers and also see why people chose to homeschool in the first place.

The book starts by showing you why homeschooling is the **best decision** you can make by sharing stories of the wonderful transformation families have seen in their children and themselves. It is worth sharing the goal because you will soon realize that everyone struggles at times to get there, and we all need a bit of help and encouragement and a realization that we are not alone in our struggles.

This first Handbook covers all the main issues you will face as a **new homeschooler**. You will find it a great source of strength to dip into when you need to remind yourself the reasons why you chose to homeschool and take inspiration from those who have gone before you.

The second Courageous Homeschooling Handbook covers more practical issues on **how to homeschool** – which method to use, advice on curriculum (and whether you need one!), how to teach children of different ages. The final volume gives **specific help** on issues we all struggle with, like how to teach math, homeschooling with dyslexia and whether to set screen time limits.

Perhaps the most difficult problem with homeschooling is **how to motivate the children**. Battles with the kids over 'school' work is one of the biggest challenges we all face and there is only space here to touch the surface.

To help you find the answer I have devoted my first highly recommended book: ***Homeschool Secrets of Success: How to avoid the battle zone*** (available worldwide on Amazon in Kindle and paperback) to tackling this problem and unlocking the key to homeschooling success.

"Having spent a small fortune on books and resources over the years, this is one book I would highly recommend to old and new home educators." ~ Amazon 5 star review

My heartfelt thanks go to all those from the Courageous Homeschooling Facebook Group, both those who I have had space to include in this Handbook and those who make the group such a delight to visit every day.

I trust their words will bring you strength and comfort and help reaffirm your resolve that teaching your child at home is the most fulfilling thing you can do.

Best wishes

Sonya

*"I am thankful for the **collective wisdom** in this Courageous Homeschooling Facebook group that stretches farther than the parameters of homeschooling. I am thankful for the lovely women in this group who are finding their voice and learning that they can be true to themselves and their families without having to cave in to the pressures of those around them who may disagree with their style of learning or parenting.*

*I am thankful for the **love** that leads the choices of this group to put family first and create a beautiful life to the best of their ability. What a lovely group we have!"*

~ Lisa, founder member,

    Courageous Homeschooling Facebook group

Sonya Chappell

Homeschooling Encouragement

When you're starting out, it's great to get strength and encouragement from those who have already taken the plunge.

What follows are just a few of the many comments which go to prove homeschooling is the best decision you ever made.

"This week I'm thankful for the **privilege** to be able to be a stay at home Mom, wouldn't trade it for anything in the world." ~ Bianka

"I'm so happy from a comment my daughter made last night. She said "**I feel so special** that I am homeschooled. I get to do special things like pen pals and field trips and stuff." I almost cried!" ~ Mandy

"I was just standing in my kitchen eating a homemade lasagne and thinking: "I really love this life" - my son is getting there, our relationship is improving, I'm enjoying time with him and hell I'm eating a lasagne I made!!! I do feel we are on a journey and this is a path that maybe we were **meant to be** on all along." ~ Lorraine x

"Looking back I should never have sent my daughter to school. She was doing so well at home. School just destroyed her confidence and took out that love of learning. She did three years and we could take no more...Given my time again **I wouldn't have sent her to school** at all." ~ Sheila

"I love the **flexibility** of homeschooling and not having to march to anyone else's beat. ...My six year old son is too far ahead now and I know he would get bored no matter how good the school was. He's used to reading what he wants, writing about what he wants, ...doing science experiments whenever he wants ...And he's used to asking questions and discussing things...and of course, he's used to playing with his little brother. School wasn't a good fit for him in the beginning and I know it definitely would not be a good fit now. I think he would hate his learning being constrained so much." ~ Ange

"The thing I like most is that we are free to work along our own schedules. I really disliked having to take my child in 5 days a week at set times. Some days I just wanted us to do something else and enjoy each others company when he was not tired from a whole day at school! **Life is too short** to give your children up to others to be raised!" ~ Saadiya

"This commitment allows your family to choose what and how your precious child will learn. You will be going back to school too. Some days you will be sure you have lost your mind. Then, suddenly you will be standing at their **graduation ceremony** wondering how it went by so fast. If the family is in agreement, it is the best, if not the biggest, investment that could ever be made on behalf of the children. My daughter is now in her first year of college...going great...I am so thankful we are a homeschool family." ~ Tess

"The way I see it is we are all doing this because **we love our children** so much and have their best interest at hearts. I think that's why in the beginning I fretted so much about what they were achieving. Now I see the results and my husband cannot believe the ideas and words that come out of his daughters' mouths sometimes...And of course my daughters are so happy." ~ Alison

"I wouldn't send my kids to school for anything. I think it is **wonderful** that you homeschool and get to enjoy each moment of their progress. I feel so much time in school is wasted waiting for the herd to settle down and listen to directions. Kids may do some critical thinking there, but they are never given time to dig deep and really follow through on what interests them.
    The other thing that bugs me is that school creates an environment of dependence on being told what to do all the time. I cannot think how this can be helpful. I understand following directions, but many in this group can attest to the fact that when their kids are pulled out of school they feel lost and directionless. They don't know what to do with

themselves. I am not suggesting that all of school is bad, but having been a product of it, I would have definitely liked to have done things differently. And I can attest to feeling that I didn't know what I wanted to do when I finished school. I headed off to college and still felt uncertain. I even finished college and never used my degree.

I just love **the freedom** that homeschooling and thinking outside the box affords us." ~ Lisa

"Hi everyone! Well it's nearly the end of our second week of homeschooling...Already I've seen **improvement** in my son's general mood and well being...It's early days but it's so lovely to see him happy and not suppressed by school life. I'm already learning SO MUCH that I'd forgotten since school....even just tonight at bed time, we've been reading a library book about physics...I'd totally forgotten about Isaac Newton and the laws of motion! I spend a lot more time googling the 1001 questions a day he asks that I can't answer! I love homeschool." ~ Steph

"We homeschool our son, aged eleven and our daughter, now nineteen, was also homeschooled. We've all had some **wonderful times** doing it and haven't regretted it for a second. My daughter is working in a job she loves and my son enjoys marine studies, nature, science, reading and playing." ~ Janet xx

"I am sitting here crying - not because I'm sad but because I am **beaming with pride**. Beaming with pride that my son - my anxious, dyslexic, dysgraphic kid is a success and it's because he did it - NOT me.

My job as a homeschool Mom - and I did it well - was to instill confidence, NEVER GIVE UP - and when I dropped him off on Monday to start his first day of school ever - 9th grade - I said: "Kick ass and take names kid!" And he laughed....YOU GOT THIS, YOU GOT THIS MOM and so does your kid!!!!" ~ Allie

"It's not about what anyone thinks, it's about you doing your best to provide a healthy learning environment... There are so many resources you can lean on, and honestly, I have learned some things right alongside my kids. Documentaries, curriculums, charter schooling online, some companies offer online classes. You don't necessarily have to be the only one teaching or helping them learn. Once kids learn to read, my philosophy is, the entire world can be opened up by books. It can be fun to plan lessons, exciting to go on field trips, and adventurous to learn about different cultures, countries and history. It can seem so overwhelming at times, but it is honestly more **rewarding** than most life experiences I've experienced anyway." ~ Jami

"Good morning everyone. Have to share with you lovely people as you've helped me so much to overcome my fears. I'm finally over school and the impact it has had on us as a family. So now we no longer have to do the same school holidays we are finally **doing our dream** visit to Maimi. Sorry guys but so excited that we can do it out of school holidays and afford it. Happy days." ~ Sharon xxx

"Just wanted to share with you all. We have

been dealing with my son's anxiety and panic attacks since kindergarten. I would put him in a brand new shirt, send him to school and by the end of the school day it was so full of holes from him chewing on it all day. At night in bed he could chew a stuffed animal to shreds. Finally I listened to my heart saying enough was enough...So at 7th grade I had enough of PS and now no more chewing on anything; no meds for anxiety...He is happy and smarter them he even realized because in PS he always kept saying: "I'm dumb." **I'm proud** of him for accomplishing what he has done. One proud homeschool Mom." ~ Connie

"So happy for you Connie that your son is so much better now than at school and that he can learn and live to his fullest potential." ~ Bianka

"Wow so you should be proud and also proud of yourself for doing what's best for your son. Well done and what an amazing journey you've been and still are on. Your journey makes me feel so much happier that I did the right thing. Big hugs to you." ~ Sharon

"I've homeschooled my four children for many years...Now the older two have **started college** so I'm at home with my younger children. We've faced all the usual uncertainties homeschooling brings but the wobbles, in hindsight I know, have all been based on irrational fears about superficial things. The reality is that I've had the opportunity and privilege to share in their lives everyday every step of the way. Their growing, their development, their awakening of themselves, all the ups and downs and I've not missed any of it. They grow up so fast anyway. I feel that home schooling has allowed me to make the most of having children and given them a calm, less pressured environment in which to unfurl." ~ Sarah

"Homeschooling means no bullying, no problems from other kids' parents, no unprofessional and degrading comments from the teacher. (When we started homeschooling) the health, confidence and happiness improvement in my daughter was there for all to see. When you look back over the journey **the progression is amazing**. If we were to be inspected that is what they would look for, progression, and for that we are as a team OUTSTANDING. Kids in school don't guarantee to get this quality. I am fortunate that when strangers ask me about homeschooling I can say I am a qualified teacher with years of experience. Understanding the issues faced in our education system is why I choose to homeschool my daughter. My daughter always backs me up by saying she learns stuff at home, she didn't in school." ~ Sheila

"I think we are so brain washed that anything other than school is wrong that we don't see the wood for the trees. I've only been on this journey a few months but bit by bit I can see how my boy has changed. My husband said to me the other night: "**I'm so proud** that you're not giving up at the first hurdle and look how happy our son is." Yes - I cried - but I feel I've been crying with happiness for weeks now ha ha." ~ Sharon

"I was quite nervous about homeschooling at first but that lasted less than a day! LOL. In just two weeks I have seen a **vast improvement** in my daughter who suddenly has a passion for learning! To be honest I didn't think this would happen so quickly! The biggest shock to me was my daughter's fear of failing! I thought for English I would sit her down to go over the first 200 words to see what ones she knew. She was so scared to get them wrong! She said the teacher would get angry if she got less than half right. Literally everything we learnt in the first few days she would panic about getting something wrong!

Another thing she told me in the first few days was that the teacher used to say to her "If you don't stop fidgeting you'll never learn anything." I know where the teacher was coming from but saying these words to a child who takes everything so literally is very damaging!! My daughter has always been on the go since she was born! People used to call her Forrest, after *Forrest Gump*, as she always ran everywhere! The **beauty** of homeschooling is that when I see her fidgeting I take her outside to do some gardening or jump on the trampoline or change the subject.

I've made her aware that math and English still need to be done but we do things in a **fun way**! In fact when we left school my daughter only knew her 2, 5 and 10 times tables. In two weeks she now knows them all! I did this by buying a times tables wall chart and two sets of pom poms (yes one for me too!). We chanted them out everyday and she loved it! I'm enjoying the beauty of getting to know my daughter more and learning what she is good at and struggles with! I did not know that my daughter could draw! In fact the art book she brought home from nearly a whole year of learning at school had four pages in it! I gave her oil pastels the other day and she drew this fairy which was incredible! I'm definitely going to encourage this!

I understand it's early days but I can hand on heart say that I feel this has been the **best decision** I've made in terms of my daughter's learning! My husband and I have said countless times how we now wish we had done it from the beginning!! We've got our **happy little girl** back who is excited to learn everyday and who tells even strangers about the experiments and different activities we've done.

Another positive is having groups like this one! I thought it was going to be a very isolating journey but I've since learnt the opposite! There are loads of support groups, educational sites, activities to go to that I've realized we are quite spoilt for choice!" ~ Kate xx

"Don't doubt yourself; you don't need qualifications to homeschool you just need to do what you have been doing all along. **No one knows your child better than you**." ~ Maria

"Having never taught my son anything, he has more scientific knowledge than all his schooled friends. Why? Because he has been allowed to **learn**, not just memorize stuff to get a sticker on a chart." ~ Jessica

"Homeschool is the courage to never settle on the hills or even the mountains: it's touching the sky, the moon, and the stars one lesson at a time. Sure, there are days of turbulence but the days of smooth sailing to the universe make up for it. For, at the end of the day, **our children** are our **best parts of this world**." ~ Callie

"Looking back over the years I had so many years where I used to worry about taking the boys our of school. So much negativity with people around us... So today I can relax knowing it was the **best decision** we ever made for our boys! They have had freedom, no pressure, and they learn because they want to learn, not because we are forcing them to.

So for all the newbies out there starting this journey, all I can say is **don't worry** about other people's opinions. You are doing this for your children's future! My boys have Aspergers and Epilepsy/Autism and they have not looked back since coming out of school." ~ Christine

A Glimpse Into Our Days

❝ I love to know what everyone else is doing I find it so inspiring." ~ Lorraine

I am including here are a few snapshots inside people's homeschool.

It will give you an insight into how different (and exciting!) your life can become once you have taken your child out of school.

You will see that wherever you live, people's homeschool days have **so much in common**. It's an exciting thought that we can reach across the ocean and touch each other's lives.

But although everyone has given permission to be quoted, not everyone likes to think that the one day they were ill is the day I've picked out!

So please read these in the generous spirit in which they have been given.

And for those who are sharing – please believe we know that this is not necessarily typical of your homeschool – because there is no such thing as a 'typical' homeschool day.

"Spellings, math, English, science and Latin are **on the menu** for today. *Worst Witch* later, chess and reading tonight. Have a good day everyone." ~ Sheila

"Morning everyone. Spending the day doing whatever comes along today. Currently **apple picker hunting**. Hope everyone has a lovely day." ~ Catherine

"We had a very **slow start** to our day with one of my children still being a bit under the weather. Unfortunately we had to cancel our fortnightly German session and we had to miss the trapeze class as well but we have decided that this week will still count as part of the holiday and we will start with all the classes again bright and breezy next week. My son has been doing some more drawing and we had a session with our electric circuit box. We have also done some reading exercises and I have been finishing reading *The Wind in the Willows* to him. He now wants to make a film where he will play *Toad* from *Toad Hall*. We also had a 'jamming session' (not sure if that what it is called, LOL) with his new drum kit he had for Christmas with lots of one legged dancing on my part and pretty cool dance moves on his part." ~ Diana

"Another wonderful plus to homeschooling! My daughter is busy writing up her values/virtues list for

philosophy. How many schools teach philosophy to seven-year-olds? My mother-in-law is blown away by the deep, meaningful conversations she can have already. I'm one happy Mommy!" ~ Alison

"We are starting work on a project to design **a home for the future** incorporating all forms of renewable energy and other ideas that may limit the damage to the environment and harness natural energy and resources." ~ Samantha

"I'm a bit **bug eyed** and have some brain fog going on; my daughter has been restless all night. She's already up playing with the kitten. Will be doing math, spelling and reading today. As of right now to the coffee pot I go." ~ Stacey

"My son is still on *Minecraft* - he's researched a tutorial and has successfully made something called a hopper! He's been practicing his typing skills by sending friend requests and I showed him how to make a cup of tea which then led to a mini conversation about tea fields in India, watching how you can change the strength and of course a rich tea dunking cookie challenge!" ~ Lorraine

"My daughter is doing a bit of **grammar** and Oceanography before we head to Fisherman's Village for some shopping and lunch with Daddy. My son is doing his usual **unschool** thing and is on his iPad. Have a great day everyone!" ~ Lisa

"We looked at **hummingbird videos**; they're so beautiful and it was wonderful to see them being hand fed. Then we looked at a video by the *Daily Woo* (!), about Walt Disney's *Dreaming Tree* and the barn in which he put on shows as a boy, all interesting stuff and you feel you've seen it in person. Have a good day, everyone." ~ Janet xx

"Good morning...We are **busy bees** today....We have already been to the shops and back for homeschool supplies....We have cleaned the downstairs toilet and fixed the toilet roll holder back on the wall, a little DIY...We stopped for a drink then my daughter started her math lesson and my other daughter and I cut up chicken for the slow cooker for tonight's tea...Then off to a farm visit with some homeschooling friends...Then we must pop into town to pick up a Nintendo *Pokémon* game. It arrived yesterday but we were too busy. At some stage I must have a sit down. Have a great day everyone." ~ Susanne

"Nice to have a glimpse into your homeschool day. Made me happy reading it. Love days like that." ~ Sarah xx

"My daughter had her first **theater performance** Friday night. It went very well! My two litte ones now want to be in theater. The theme was *The Man Behind The Mask*. The children studied what it takes to become a character while wearing makeup or masks. Today we are running errands and preparing for Thanksgiving. We'll do a craft and bake. Have a lovely day!" ~ Danielle

"It's turned out to be a nice day if somewhat windy so skipping the formal sit down lessons and going outside to **enjoy the sunshine**." ~ Kaitlin

"We are doing great! We have been traveling in Italy, Switzerland and next is France, Spain and Portugal. We had a nice day today visiting more **churches and castles**." ~ Monica

"My daughter has a **piano lesson** this morning and in between she will be doing her normal routine of spellings, reading, math problems and French homework this afternoon followed by some Lego time. This evening she has her tap dancing lesson with her sister. My son is working on math and English this morning - finishing off French homework and then baking this afternoon. Tonight is drama rehearsals for their October show "*Oliver*" and Saturday is packed with singing lessons, ballet and musical theater. Have a great weekend everyone." ~ Anni x

"We are waiting for our math and English **tutor** to arrive to cover any areas the girls need help. Later friends are coming over for lunch and social. We made macaroni cheese, we have pizza, salad and garlic bread. Looks like a fabulous day in the making." ~ Susanne

"Morning everyone. Hope you're all having good days so far. We have been doing **arts and crafts** this morning and the girls are currently in the middle of their kickboxing lesson. After a spot of lunch we will be having an afternoon of science and baking." ~ Samie

"At 9am my eldest (six-years-old) grabbed an **empty box** and decided to make a TV out of it. She crawled in and started reading a news broadcast. It was hilarious. Soon after her little sisters made TVs too. Weather reports, TV shows, thrillers, *My Little Pony* news - I've had it all! They even wrote an episode of *Poldark* for me! And made remote controls and wrote out TV guides.... Six hours later and they're still being creative with these boxes. I did have a space session planned for today but I chose to get out of their way. If my daughter went to school she certainly wouldn't have been afforded the time and space to come up with the idea, never mind see it through. What a **fantastic day** of bonding and creativity for them. Feeling very positive today about the choice we have made." ~ Penny

"Happy Tuesday everyone. It's a miserable day here, so we've spent the morning at the **library**. I wanted to escape the house but our options are limited with all this rain! We'll do some reading later and perhaps some math on the iPads. Quite a lazy day today." ~ Cathy x

"Today we are doing some **cooking** and my son has his guitar lesson. He has also started a course on game design - another of his great passions, along with animation." ~ Maria x

"Today I have very proud **bantam chicken breeders** age 10 and 14, who unknowingly are completing a project on biology, business, budgeting, carpentry, basic animal care and photography." ~ Lunar

"Good morning! I'm spinning with ideas and I love when I get this way as I get to planning fun learning opportunities for my unschooled. My son has shown interest lately in becoming a **police officer**. Although he's only five we are arranging a visit with the police station and tour of the armory and car. Both my in-laws work there so we have some insider help.

We also have a stuffed animal with a tore lip! Kids say he is vomiting cotton and needs surgery so we will have a lesson in sewing and health. Gotta take advantage of every opportunity right? We also are planning to continue our study of endangered animals. Both kids wanted to work on it at midnight last evening but Mama was too tired. Have a great day!" ~ Mandy

"Our family has started a new homeschool adventure. We just bought a 5th wheel and we are going to be **traveling around the US** and learning as we go. My son is profoundly deaf and very hands-on, so right now we are in the desert. We are learning about the land, and animal tracks today, while playing in the sand." ~ Sonia

"Good morning! Today we are following the daily schedule and playing some **math games**. I am also scanning all the books I use for teaching and finishing laminating some self-correcting math cards that I printed yesterday... I need some holidays!" ~ Maria

"This morning **bird watching** down the park. Afraid to say they got carried away in the park and we forgot the bird watching! Came home and looked up bird nests on the computer. Watched a cartoon character telling us about bird nests. Drew a bird and nest on the blackboard. Next task buy some food for the birds tonight as they will be cold. P.S. Sang '*The North Wind Shall Blow*' for the first time in years." ~ Vicki

"We are **cake baking** for my Dad's 70th do on Saturday." ~ Mandy

"We are missing our homeschooled group today as we are heading out to a **plumbing expo** with Dad out of town. Dad will be 'teacher' while maybe I get some time at a different fabric store! Our new fun thing we are doing is watching the behavior of wasps/hornets. We have a box on our window for birds to build a nest in with the protective film so we can see them but they can't see us or be disturbed by our lights. No birds have ever used it but the other day a pair of wasps showed up and have built one section of a nest. We've watched them sleep, which is really cute, if you can believe that. They do a lot of walking around and possibly courting, we haven't researched that yet. It's interesting, though is quite a distraction from their math work." ~ Shelley

"My husband left early this morning for a work trip, so I've enjoyed some time alone reading this morning while the children had their **tablet time**. Now it's about time for getting up, dressed and fed before the cleaners come. My eldest has Cubs tonight so we'll all be up late which means giving the two-year-old a rare nap during the day (not much sleeping last night so this should be easy!) during which I plan to start weightlifting - been planning this for a while but not actually starting so it will be good to get going! Not too much else on, Monday is usually a quiet day, so we'll probably just start a new read-aloud together, and my daughter will get on with something for her artist's badge at Cubs." ~ Katie

"I think we are going to head down to the **craggy cliffs** and read a chapter of *Smugglers Cove* with a hot chocolate. I've cancelled the usual 'quick rush to homeschool gymnastics' after deciding I need to do things that I like too!!" ~ Sarah

"Goooood morning - and it's a really beautiful day here! Today we are **hitting the books** this morning; math, handwriting and computer science, then a science experiment. Then we are visiting the grandparents and going horse riding - hopefully out in the sunshine....

We all have different ideas on what we want our homeschool to look like, but if we all just take it easy and remember there is **learning in everything** our children do I am sure we will all be doing great!" ~ Becky

Starting Out

Top Tips For New Homeschoolers

I asked my 10,000+ homeschool fans and members of the Courageous Homeschooling Facebook Group to share their top tips for new homeschoolers starting out.

It's always good to see what traps others have fallen into so you know what to avoid!

"Relax. **Don't compare.** Not to public school, not to other homeschool families... Do what works for you and your children. That's the beauty of homeschooling. I promise, even when you think you're doing it all wrong, or not doing enough, you will see your children growing and learning. It's amazing." ~ Jennifer

"**Deschool** if you've deregistered. Don't jump in with both feet. Take time to get to know each other again. Don't try to recreate school at home and don't go out buying every single resource without looking for free ones first." ~ Emma

"Don't look at it as a full school time commitment. **Take one year at a time**, and plan that way. Next year you could be in a totally different place. And a different thing could work that doesn't work now. Also, every kid is different. What works for one doesn't always work for the other. Do what works for your family *right now.* Figure next year out next year." ~ Monica

"Find a **friend** who you can moan to who won't suggest you put them back into school." ~ Jessica

"Take **breaks** when you need to or when the kids need to, don't make it hell, ask for your kids input of what they want to know about, and talk/discuss out loud more than you write on paper." ~ Samantha

"Learning comes in many forms, not just at a desk with a book being talked down to. Explore all of the forms. Forget what you thought you knew, indulge in a major mind shift. See it as a **lifestyle**. Connection with family members is crucial, let that be your priority, the other stuff will follow. If something ain't working change it up or toss it out. Happiness and health all round are conducive to much learning. Find your family rhythm, there are no *have-to's* unless you set the *have-to's*. Have fun, be silly, laugh, love, live the example of lifelong learning. Take breaks. Have holidays. Get out and explore the world around you. Pray pray pray. It's an incredible magical journey." ~ Kim

"Take your time!!!! You will never be at the same place as anyone else and that's good. ABOVE ALL if you are frustrated take a day off. We have taken multiple days off because of burn out on the kids. It's Okay you will find your niche and once you do it's amazing." ~ Peggy

"Don't try to be **perfect**." ~ Amanda

"Invest in a **planner** that you love, but is also efficient for your needs. A good planner that is easy to use, whether store-bought, online, or home-made, can be a god-send. Bookshelves are also a good investment. Even though you can't fill them now, those books are mighty sneaky, and you'll be drowning before you know it. Plus. You can never have too many pencils!" ~ Samantha

"**Later** is better." ~ Laurie

"**Don't worry about curriculum**. Just fill in gaps and teach through life lessons. You will come across curricula as you get more involved and find one that is suited for your child." ~ Serene

"Take it **one moment** at a time." ~ Heather

"Looking back I wish I had spend less time worrying and more time trying, failing and **laughing** about it." ~ Stine

"Do what you do and **tune out the naysayers**, because their arguments are based on what they've been taught to say, not actual life experience-- which is the best part of homeschooling, experiencing life." ~ Arleene

"You're allowed to have **days off**. You're allowed to dummy spit. You're allowed to change without notice. You love your kids and have their best interests at heart so you won't ruin them!" ~ Diana

"Remember to infuse **fun** into your schooling. It doesn't have to look like a public school setting. Make sure to weave your child/children's favorite things into the curriculum." ~ Tracie

"Ask for advice. But don't be afraid to ask several different people, get several different answers, then do some research to form your own educated opinion, and do it the way it works for you and your child. Everyone is **different**, and that's Okay!" ~ Beth

"Being nervous and scared is Okay! We've all been there and will go through our moments of doubts. You just take **one day at a time**, and once you have a little confidence, it helps you push on...There are so many sources available to help them learn in the subjects they love, even if you feel you're not up to the task. Don't feel discouraged." ~ Danielle

"Relax and **enjoy**." ~ Tiffany

"Go with the flow, don't try to be perfect and notice what is working and what isn't. Be prepared to totally **change approach** where needed and be adaptable." ~ April

"Listen to what others have to say, but in the end DO IT YOUR WAY. You know your children better than anyone else, do what fits them and you best." ~ Jenny

"**Breathe**!! You've got what it takes! God gave them to you to love, raise, and teach!" ~ Margaret

"Take people's comments with a pinch of salt. People like to share all the good things but they too struggle, you aren't alone. Spend lots of time just **getting to know** your children and what they enjoy. I was shocked at how little I knew my children and how little they really knew themselves when we removed them from school. We took lots of time out just playing and doing fun tasks getting to know each other.

Leave those groups full of judgmental people who insist you have to homeshool in a certain way. **Trust yourself**, you do know what is best for your family. There are groups that will support you however you decide to educate your children.

Don't rush into joining every subscription or start stock piling resources. It's amazing how little you actually need and how much just gets left on the shelf. There are also many homeschool groups that source great **discounts** on subscriptions as well as groups for sharing resources. Homeschooling really doesn't have to cost much, we actually spend less on resources now than if our children were in school." ~ Ruth

"It's normal to feel fear in the beginning but the trick is to **feel the fear and do it anyway**." ~ Samantha

"Relax and breathe, it's **not a race** and doesn't have to fit other's standards, just your own." ~ Brianne

"What I perceive as perfect style of learning is not always what my kids think is perfect! Go with the flow, don't model public school and take one day at a time. The first year is a learning curve for the whole family. Utilize thrift stores for games and books to save money." ~ Mandy

"Buy plenty of **wine**." ~ Vicky

"I wish I would have read all of these **before** we embarked on this journey. It would have saved many tears and our first year from being World War Three in my house! Despite the hardships, we are now going into our 7th year of homeschooling." ~ Lindsay

Why Do People Choose To Homeschool?

❝ The final straw for me was when after loads of meetings with the school they threatened to fine me because my child was frightened to go to school and felt unsafe. In front of me the attendance officer told my eleven year old son: "No one died from a punch and we all get bullied." To this day I don't know how I walked out of there without punching her.

I vowed that minute no more. Our children have no chance with people like that in the system. I came home and cried and cried and then thought NO my child will not be made to feel he has to put up with bullying. The look of **pure relief** on his face when I said he didn't have to go back will stay with me forever." ~ Sharon x

"Hi, my name is Sonia, and I am from Texas. I have four children, but three of them are now adults. I started homeschooling my three older kids because one of them was labeled '**learning disabled**' by the school they were attending. He

43

was having a hard time, so I took all three out of school. We enjoyed learning at home a lot, and as my youngest started college, we welcomed a new baby boy into our family. Our youngest is now seven-years-old, and has never been to a school.

Our homeschooling experience has changed a great deal over the years, and each child has been taught very **differently**. With each child bringing new challenges, our youngest is profoundly deaf, we have had to learn and change as we all learn to communicate and find new and unique ways of learning together." ~ Sonia

"My 12-year-old is 'behind' in school terms, but now thriving at home...She probably has dyslexia, and she also was a three months premature baby, took a virus, and ended up being airlifted for intensive life support. School did not work for her, she is such a **playful child**, with a lot of playing to make up for after being in a coma for the first six months... I couldn't stand to see her suffer in school, and regret it took me so long to learn the law here. Now she is thriving and her natural intelligence and joy and creativity can really shine." ~ Dawn

"My son struggled with reading in public school. He was getting extra help, but the school was pulling him out of **all the fun things** for it. He was missing out on art, music, etc... One day I asked how his day was and my first grader said: "Nothing is fun about school." I was done and started researching homeschool...Four years in, he's an excellent reader and a happy boy." ~ Amanda

"When my oldest was about to start school, we

took her to see her potential class and meet the teacher, and she completely **shut down**. Even the sparkly glitter shoes that, at home, she couldn't get enough of, she ignored. Just being there, my highly animated preschooler was suddenly comatose. Then we discovered if she rode the bus, she would have to make a transfer, and she was tiny compared to others her age.

God prepared us for that moment. We knew we didn't have to accept this. Turned out this was a **great choice**. She was not a reader until third grade, but then caught up to 'grade level' and beyond by the end of the year! Public school would have held her back in SO many ways. The one year she was in public school due to complications at home, she had straight 'A's and blew the teachers away." ~ Wanita

"The kicker was my oldest son's 1st grade teacher not allowing him to use the bathroom after telling her he had urinary tract issues which required surgery and he needed to be allowed to go to the bathroom at all times... Also, he was so **ahead of the class** it was a waste of everyone's time and he was so unhappy there. He seemed to be in mourning even though his life was steady and stable. After just a short time at home we re-found our boy that we always knew was buried underneath all that stress and torment. Now after fourteen years I have a long list of reasons to homeschool. It makes me sad that it took something so sad to wake me up to the awful situation." ~ Katherine

"I had three children in the public school system. Two of them were being **bullied** and the admin were turning a blind eye to it. After my youngest was given lunch detention after defending himself against a physical assault and the bully who started it got no punishment, I pulled all three out that very day." ~ Brandy

"(We homeschool) because the school district we were in was grossly overcrowded. The students were disrespectful and mean. The principal told me that they didn't have one second available to devote to teaching manners and good conduct. They started practicing for **standardized tests** four months in advance and had a practice test four days a week. My son was exhausted mentally, physically, and emotionally...I was done. He was done. We took two weeks off to decompress, started homeschooling and **never looked back**." ~ Gina

"We started after my eldest started in mainstream and was bullied while the head mistress turned a blind eye to keep her school's Academy status. I removed him in frustration for the system failure. I now realize that the whole system is wrong. I homeschool to give my children the best **well rounded education** I can and they deserve. The teachers are not the problem – it's the rules they are bound by." ~ Kailey-Jane

"My oldest never finished 3rd grade...The class as a whole was two to three months behind at the end of the year (but) there was no time for the school to go back and cover what was missed. When I asked how this was going to affect the pupils I was basically told by the teacher that she couldn't go back because **she had a schedule** and it was her job to follow that no matter what. We pulled our kids the next day." ~ Becky

"Sent my now nine-year-old to public though I didn't want to...He hated it. Not sure exactly what set him off but he wouldn't stand just being dropped off and told to hang in there despite all our attempts. He finally just said "Dad, why can't moms and dads just teach their kids letters and numbers?"...(In the end I decided) I wouldn't throw my **baby lamb** to the wolves and yanked him out." ~ Nom

"(I homeschool one of my children who was diagnosed with ADHD). I knew public school wouldn't be a place for him to **thrive**. Filling out pages of busy work, sitting still, 26:1 student teacher ratio and having the same expectations placed on him as a 'normal' student would only end up with him feeling like a failure. So halfway through 3rd grade we pulled him. And we're still going after two years." ~ Amy

"Simple answer is because of my son being constantly bullied and then punished for doing nothing wrong." ~ Lucy

"My daughter is four and was attending a regular preschool academy until she was diagnosed with a sensory disorder with ADHD symptoms by the school itself. Mild behaviors seemed to be the focus of the educator and not that fact that my daughter at only four is reading and obviously very **gifted**. I don't want to let the stigma of being different in any way to hold my child back. I want her to feel loved and supported, and thus we have begun our journey towards homeschooling." ~ Meadow

"I have an eight year old son who was diagnosed with autism and an 18 month old son. I recently decided to pull my eight-year-old from a Canadian school after a long struggle to get him support in the classroom. They do not provide sufficient funding for special education programs and I saw him getting left behind. He is doing well at home much more happier than when he was in school...The **public school system has failed him** and so many other children. I love homeschooling my boys." ~ Rebekah

"Rebekah I know many others feel like you do! I am always struck with this statistic: Only 19% of parents of children on the autism spectrum felt that their children were receiving education to adequately prepare them for life, compared to 56% of parents of children without disabilities." ~ Sonya

"I started to think about homeschooling since I started discovering my elder daughter's **gifts**. A lot of reading about giftedness led me to decide on unschooling in the early childhood and homeschooling later on." ~ Shazia

"(Why did I take my child our of school?)...It has to do with the **entire package**. The anxiety a child encounters due to the bullies, the excessive amount of work, the competitiveness, the teachers that aren't there to teach, crappy food, hardly any fresh air....Oh boy, I could go on and on. One of the biggies.....socialization...haha. Yes, it's socialization

when your child sits behind a desk for hours, unable to talk with the same bunch of kids they knew since childhood. That one kills me. Where is the logic in public school? It's a babysitting service. Wow...this post put me in a mood. LOL. Hey, I'm going to the New York state museum this morning with the kids."
~ Nikki

Let's end with this encouraging comment from Beth:

"For me, the hardest part was making the decision to homeschool. After that, you've **got it**." ~ Beth

Sonya Chappell

Can I Cope?

When you are beginning homeschool we all face the same AGH! moment.

Can you do this? Will your child miss out?
Sharon asks the question which is on all of our lips:

"**Hello everybody. I'm struggling to know where to start and finding the whole thing worrying. What if I can't teach my son as well as a school and not get him up to standard for his exams? Sorry to be negative I'm just feeling out of my depth. On the other hand my son is back to his funny happy self which just makes me so happy. But is that enough**?" ~ Sharon

"I'd say the first thing you have to do is stop thinking that you have to **teach** him. Schools teach...but kids invariably don't learn from teaching. Try to think of yourself as a facilitator, then you're on the right track. Kids learn from finding out for themselves. Sit down and have a really good talk about what he wants to learn and how he's gonna do it. Take him to the library, show him how to safely surf the net and search YouTube. And don't forget to deschool. Hth." ~ Rachel

"(I am a qualified teacher) and I am only one out of SO MANY teachers out there that turn to homeschooling to educate their kids instead of sending them to traditional school. And it is so true that you **don't need a degree** to teach your kids! I don't feel like I'm insulting teachers by saying that or devaluing myself. I have met teachers with degrees who should not have been teaching plain and simple so that piece of paper meant nothing! I think teaching is an art and I know I don't know everything there is to know about that art even with a degree, but I know how to look stuff up and anyone else who can read and is so inclined can do that too!" ~ Ange

"Despite what the school says, not a single teacher has a degree in every subject! School can be an awful place.... They will likely never recommend homeschool. But there are loads of **resources** from schooling online to creating your own curriculum to even unschooling. If you have questions, we are here for you!" ~ Lisa

"Thank you. I go from being really positive to really scared in the space of a day ha ha. I think its peoples' attitudes that get me. They say how can you teach him if you don't know what to do yourself?" ~ Sharon xx

"I have only been homeschooling my twin 11-year-olds for two weeks. Day one was a nightmare because I enrolled with K12/CAVA and the curriculum as well of the amount of work they expected kids to do in one day was outrageous! I was stressed and they were miserable!! Thankfully I went to a local homeschool park day and the support from other Moms was amazing!! All of the above was said and was greatly appreciated! We are doing the **right thing** and don't doubt it for one moment!! Our kids are little for a short time. Our job is to make sure they are happy. Everything else will come. The more time they spend with us the better. They are learning by example. Hang in there!!" ~ Yvette

"There's no getting away from the fact that it can be challenging being with the same people day in, day out, but we have found that our relationship with our children is less challenging and filled with more **love and joy** compared to the war zone it felt like we were living when they were attending school. We find its important to make sure there are ways to always have some time to be able to go and be yourself away from the children to do something just for us. It's important to keep your own identity and sanity. Groups and the friendships we have formed over the years also help massively with keeping us sane as we're all in the **same boat** together." ~ Erika

"I was the same as you, worried I wouldn't be able to teach my son things he needs to know but you can find most of what you need **online** (even old exam papers) and if there is anything you or your son don't understand 90% of the time you can find a YouTube video that explains it. My son's confidence is so much better now and things the school said he was behind with he is now advanced on. Children learn in different ways and you know your son better than anyone so don't doubt yourself you will do fine." ~ Maria x

"Thank you Maria. You're right I'm getting to know him so much more now and loving the time with him and not rushing around all the time." ~ Sharon x

"You can get him where he needs to be. First - dust off what the "school way" is. Forget about it. Learning is innate and you both just need to find it. As far as making sure he's on point, I am very flexible but I am a stickler for math and my kids happen to enjoy it so we use Khan academy for math and they are all on or above grade level. It's self paced - if they know something they don't need endless hours of repetition or if they don't understand they watch the video and practice more. There are tons of **free courses** you can take online in any subject area and Khan also has many subject areas well besides math to choose from. Online is your friend, and the library etc. Experiential learning is great too. Do what works for you but you can do it - children often learn better out of school than within." ~ Allie

"I know how you feel, Sharon. My eldest went to public school from age four to age 12. She had already started her second year in high school last September, when we finally decided enough is enough after years and years of bullying, even after changing schools a few times. The first couple of months weren't easy. My daughter was struggling to get used to a more relaxed atmosphere and if it wasn't her, it was me panicking about whether I could teach a high school aged child. I had already been homeschooling the two younger ones. We then decided to **unschool** for a couple of months before Christmas with all three kids.

It really helped, although I often panicked again, because we weren't doing any "school work." After Christmas we were all ready to add some structure. One of the biggest problems my eldest had after leaving the public school, was initiative. She was so used to being told what to do and what to think and "being fed everything like a baby." She would struggle to relax and always feel this terrible stress to HAVE to do something resembling school, but seemed to resent the worksheets or books I would give her.

Now, she gets up in the morning, grabs some breakfast and sits down with it and some workbooks and starts working, without me having to say anything to her at all. Do I still worry about her education? Sometimes, I think we all do though. It is only natural, as we want the best for them. But most of the time I am happy we made that choice, as I know, that by home schooling her, she will have the chance to do and become **anything she wants**. Hang in there." ~ Simone

I Feel So Overwhelmed

"I'm considering not sending my nearly four-year-old to school this September and I also have a eight-year-old at school.

My dream is to homeschool both but I'm worried I won't be able to teach them what they need and I will find it overwhelming.

I have this feeling I'm doing something bad which I know is because I'm going against the norm. Did anyone else feel like this before?" ~ Laura

"Laura this is absolutely the right place to ask questions and blow away those anxieties. Of course you can do this. Homeschooling is a **natural extension** of parenting and there are all sorts of online resources you can use for any bits you are unsure of but at this level I am sure you'll be just fine." ~ Sheila

"Hi Laura. Yes, I felt weird about homeschooling at first. Homeschooling was something I never planned to do, I was a teacher and so I kind of just

57

automatically thought I would send my kids to school.

However, my son had a bad experience at kindergarten (the teachers wouldn't take him to the toilet when he asked and he wet himself and they didn't let him paint what he wanted, they wouldn't let me stay even just a few moments to make sure he was settled, along with a few other things that just didn't sit well with me and set him up to love learning at such a young age) so I just pulled him out.

I started looking at homeschooling, kind of resigning myself to it just for the time we were going to be in India, but you know what? The more I read about homeschooling the more I couldn't believe it sort of WASN'T **the norm**. I mean people have their reasons for not homeschooling obviously, but basically, I believe me being uncomfortable with it to begin with, and why so many other people are anti-homeschooling, is simply because if you haven't been exposed to it you sort of just have this narrow world view about it. If you went to school and your parents went to school, all your friends went to school, you might think that school's the only way to get an education. It's clearly not.

Anyway, so now I don't know if we'll ever send our kids to public school because I see the benefits of homeschooling first hand. It's just so efficient in many ways. And Okay, I was a teacher, but you DO NOT have to have a teaching degree to teach your children. I use boxed curricula mostly. There are so many **great resources** out there and ways to homeschool cheaply, and I think children just really thrive with freedom and quiet and someone around to actually discuss ideas with instead of just being told to keep quiet. I have a thirteen-year-old nephew who has been to public school all his life and he struggles to read and my son is six and reading at a high school level.

Every homeschooling family is different, every child is different and so if you are thinking of homeschooling you have to **trust** that and not worry if you aren't 'keeping up'. We do have days when we don't get much done but other days we learn SO much. We follow a loose schedule and my son knows what that is and I try to make learning enjoyable as much as I can, give him breaks when I can clearly see he's fading from hunger or fatigue or whatever, listen to his ideas about how he wants to approach his learning, so we really don't have that many battles.

Having said that, my son is not used to the school system so you might need to spend some time **deschooling** and whatnot. This group – the Courageous Homeschooling group - is great to be part of. We all want to help. We all need each other. Homeschooling won't be easy but sending kids to public school isn't exactly easy either. At the end of the day, if this is what you want and need for your kids, you can do this!" ~ Ange

"Thank you, my oldest is eight and for all of a year and a half...she had toilet accidents and the teachers would never notice all day and she wouldn't say anything. She is happy in school now but I don't want to put my littlest through anything like that." ~ Laura

"Laura - I am glad you posted because I have been feeling the same concerns. And seeing the encouraging posts from others has helped me too. Good luck!" ~ Annette

"It all seems a lot harder and worse now because

it is all new. You will feel very different down the road a bit, and your child will be thanking you! Their life and yours are about to change for the **better!** You will both finally get some peace. You've got this and we are here cheering you on!" ~ Lisa

"I think most of us feel overwhelmed at some point, especially at first. I did! Hence I started home educating our youngest, then decided to do the same with the middle one and some months later our eldest, too. Up until recently, I would still worry, because the eldest is so close to exams, compared to the other two. I read Sonya's book **Homeschool Secrets of Success** the other day and I wish I had read it sooner. It is so reassuring, for any stage of homeschooling, any age of children. I really can only recommend it, if you haven't read it yet. As everybody else has already said, you can do it!!!" ~ Simone

"Yeah. Mine have all been homeschooled, started almost 15 years ago when my daughter was three. Over the years, I've been criticized and even mocked by family. Once, when my Mom visited as we were out to breakfast, my oldest boy made a silverware statue, and she said kind of meanly: "So, does this count as science now?"
Some people don't get that we want the **best** for our children, and many of us don't think the best is public school. It's not about what anyone thinks, it's about you doing your best to provide a healthy learning environment for them. There are so many resources you can lean on, and honestly, I have learned some things right alongside my kids. Documentaries, curriculums, charter schooling online, some companies offer online classes with help keeping track of grades and accomplishments.

You don't necessarily have to be the only one teaching or helping them learn.

Once kids learn to read, my philosophy is, the entire world can be opened up by books. It can be fun to plan lessons, exciting to go on field trips, and adventurous to learn about different cultures, countries, and history. It can seem so overwhelming at times, but it is honestly **more rewarding** than most life experiences I've experienced anyway. My kids have a natural desire to learn; they enjoy it. I think that's far more common for kids that learn at home versus kids in public schools. I think it's normal to feel overwhelmed at times. I hope that helps." ~ Jami

"Hi Laura. Don't worry you CAN DO THIS but, just like parenting, homeschooling is not an instant fix. It's more like a **marathon**. It takes quite a time to work out what method suits both you and your children; we all vary in how we do it – some of us run basically a school at home and others of us are totally unstructured and going with the flow. If there is a theme, it is that almost always people grow more **relaxed** on scheduling as time goes on and they gain confidence that actually learning is not something which is always measured by workbooks. Good luck and do come back here for support and encouragement when you need it." ~ Sonya x

"Hi, I started homeschooling my twelve year old son this past November. He went to public school until the seventh grade. I just keep thinking, I hope I don't mess him up... LOL... I am very nervous about everything... I want so badly for him to do well and I'm always praying that I can teach him well enough so he can graduate. I often think I'm not teaching him all that he needs to know.. Thank you so much for taking the time to try and help terrified parents, like me, feel more **confident** that we made the right choice." ~ Buddy and Kathy

Too Many Subjects To Teach

❝I just wondered does anyone else sometimes feel really overwelmed with all the subjects etc.?

Today I ended up getting myself in a state and saying to my 12-year-old, "I think you will do better in school because we (yes I said 'we') are not doing a very good job."

We have been for a lovely dog walk to clear our heads and he's now getting on with his topic work while I sit looking at him feeling like the worst Mom ever." ~ Sharon

"Sharon, hang on in there! We all get days like this hun and this is exactly the place to air your concerns and frustrations where we can support each other. You are providing an amazing **opportunity** for your child. He would never get this level of one-to-one attention in school. If you feel overwhelmed, take a break and when you are ready have another look at your plan. If you plan loads in a day and you don't complete it all, you are setting yourself up to fail. Why not just try a couple of subjects a day? Also take stock once a week or once a month. Then you'll get a clearer picture of progression. It's 1.20pm here and we haven't even started work yet. Record achievements in a draft e-mail then look back at them at the end of a week. Take a break, relax and rebuild. Big hugs." ~ Sheila

"Thank you so much Sheila. What you say makes so much sense. I sometimes see what other people are doing and feel envious that they have it so together and sound like they are doing amazing, when some days I could cry. I have it in my head that if we don't do well when it comes to exams later on then I will have failed him. And that he's missing out on more than I can give him. I go to bed worrying and wake up worrying." ~ Sharon xxxxx

"It's natural to worry and we all have 'sod it' days! Don't fight it. Go with the flow and look at the bigger picture. Exams aren't everything but I understand what you mean about preparing your child for life. I am very sure you are **not failing him**. Schedule some personal project time for him too, let him pursue an interest, it will give him ownership and you some time too." ~ Sheila

"Thank you. You've made me feel a lot better. I'm going to have a cup of tea and chill out." ~ Sharon xxxx

"Don't feel bad hun. We've all been there. Oh the tantrums I used to have. Draw a line under it and get on with **learning at his pace**." ~ Rachel xx

"You're not being negative. You're venting about the struggle. No different than when I worked in the schools and had a team meeting. You gain **strength** from your colleagues.

Meanwhile, relax a bit. All the subjects you say? You don't have to cover them daily - or weekly, even. Your day doesn't have to resemble school in any way and you can still end up with literate, educated, independent humans that are kind and know how to manage their time. Don't be afraid to **change things up**. If in school, there is 10 to 15 minutes of instruction and then the kids do their thing. We were in public first. I tried to replicate the school day and at about the four or five month mark I was in your shoes.

I dumped the whole thing and began asking what the **kids wanted to do**. They wanted to play. Okay...so we played chess, we baked (great math, that's how my kids learned fractions), we went to museums and we had fun. They were 1st, 2nd, and 4th. Then we discovered their passions. Oldest loved history. So he watched documentaries and he read everything he could find on the topic of WWI and WWII. As they got older, we added in Khan Academy. They logged into math and they loved it. They use it for computer programming. There is a grammar, music, etc., section. We became rather unschooly.

For us I've got an 8th grader who is going to high school and he's **not behind** after being unschooled for five years. He learned how to write a persuasive essay just in January. He's on point for math. His love of history and geography and social studies has put him ahead. It's all relative. We used to live in a state that had more requirements but we still taught like this....I just learned educational-ease and wrote things up well. You can get through this hump.

Crash course science /history on YouTube is great. A twelve-year-old boy will think he won the lottery if allowed to watch YouTube. These shows are fun and educational and presented by real scientists and historians with a blast of comedy. They are fast and catchy and the information sticks.

Don't be afraid to take some time off from traditional learning. It's called deschooling. You got this." ~ Allie

"You are so so right. Because we have done primary and the dreaded SATS (UK standard assessment tests) I suppose I'm still in school mode and I don't want to admit it but yes I still try to stick to a school day (I've even said 'you wouldn't do that in school.') I'm in the bubble of getting in five or six double subjects a day. And yes it's overwhelming me so it must be worse for my son. I really am into: "What will people think of me?" So from this exact minute I will stop. Thank you for taking the time to advise me. Much appreciated." ~ Sharon xxxx

"I was told to do only **90 minutes a day** if doing actual school work for middle school and max. of two and a half hours a day for high school. It's all relative and yes, you're in the public school mindset. Let it all wash away. It'll be Okay. In fact it'll be better. You grab a book, relax and read. He will read too. We changed up bedtimes. They could read until whenever. They slept in and grew. I swear public schooled kids grow more in summer or over breaks because they sleep more then. My kids began to grow anytime they needed more sleep. You're great. **You're amazing** and try different things 'til you find what works for your child. Just breathe. He'll be fine." ~ Allie

"You make perfect sense and I really do feel so much better thank you. We are made to jump through hoops and be a certain standard at a certain age and if you do not get up to that standard you are classed as below average. How does that make a child feel? It's so sad. The ones who are above average get all the praise and attention and it's so so wrong." ~ Sharon

"Oh my.....I've been there so many times. We are not perfect parents. We need to stop being so hard on ourselves and understand we are so very **blessed** to even be in a position as to homeschool. Take a day off, heck, take a few days off and breathe. I'm on the go 24/7 and when I sit, I feel so guilty. I am retraining my thought process. I am a sensitive person who puts so much pressure on herself, I make myself sick. You are doing great Mama. You will always have us here to support you along the way." ~ Nikki

"Thank you Nikki. You're right I need to look at the positives instead of the negatives and realize just how blessed we are and the reasons we started our journey. Thank you." ~ Sharon xxxx

"Every day I used to wonder if I've failed my grandson. If somehow he's been shortchanged.

Then we begin to talk. About life and how math helps with that - money and measurements and time. We use it to improve our lives, not to pass a test. We talk about history and the mistakes made in the past and how that can show us a better way for the future. We discuss grammar and how it is used to create more effective communication. And then I know that he is **learning all the time**. Not just memorizing to get the test score that will let him move on to the next thing to memorize, but really learning. And so am I. Don't judge yourself by the system that has already failed him. You can do this and you don't have to do it any way except the way that works for him to learn." ~ Harriet

"Awww Harriet you've set me off crying. LOL. In a lovely way because I know you are 100% correct. Before I de-registered our house was sad because our son was so unhappy and scared. Five months on he's so funny and always singing and laughing and every single day he tells me I'm the best Mom ever." ~ Sharon

"Sharon I so understand your fears. But what the schools call education (in the US anyway) is more like brainwashing at times. I have some teacher friends who are amazing, but they are constrained by a system that teaches to the test. They try so hard, but they are limited in resources. That means that anyone who's a little outside of the box gets stuck just trying to survive the system - forget learning. **We're doing Okay**, you and I. Our kids are learning how to learn and that's about the most important thing we can give them!" ~ Harriet

"You are a very lovely wise person and thank you for making me see what's in front of me. My boy is happy and learning life skills and number one he's safe. I didn't ever think I would be in this position but now that I am I'm going to make the best of it and enjoy it. Thank you." ~ Sharon xxx

"Hang in there. It's easy to get overwhelmed. I started three months ago. When we first started our energy was so high and I worked hard to fill four hours of activities for my five and seven-year-old. Looking back I guess I was trying to mimic public also. We have to remember the **big picture** and why we started to home educate in the first place. I never think to put them back in public. Know the first year is the hardest. I've been more laid back and although I have guilty feelings I know my kids are learning. What is your main goal? Mine is to make learning fun. Try doing science and history once or twice a week. Read aloud everyday, go easy on yourself. You are doing more for them than public would. Take a reset if needed." ~ Mandy

"Thank you. I'm going to sit back and chat with my son and work with him instead of just setting loads of work and wanting it done in a certain time. I think I've finally realized the whole point is NOT school. LOL. I'm going to write our hopes and goals down and take it from there." ~ Sharon x

"Sharon I also have a 12-year-old and I know how challenging it can be homeschooling a soon want to be independent *tween*. In our first year we did only four days and we extended the school year

69

a bit longer so we could complete our goals. Not to mention we had a lot of backup work because he had lots of medical appointments that year. We are in our third year and things are definitely a lot better. In our home, we do about 50% of the work on the computer and the other 50% on paper or workbooks. Explore his/her interests and plan together. This is a **learning experience** for both of you. You'll see the change." ~ Maria

"Thank you Maria. I love the term tween I'm going to be saying that a lot ha ha. Now I've got my head straight and stop trying to school like school I'm sure I will get better. I need to stop clock watching too (that's what I'm so bad at.)   I also need to stop stressing as I'm sure it affects my son too. Thanks again." ~ Sharon xxxx

"There are lots of ups and downs with homeschooling. I feel like a bad parent when my kids are struggling or not paying attention. But that moment when you are present to see **the light come on** in their eyes and they have figured something out...it makes up for all the struggle. I love getting to witness that firsthand, not reading it on a report card. It's the best feeling!" ~ Angie

"That's lovely Angie and how I feel and it's nice to know I'm not alone. You are so right we love them so much and want everything to be perfect for them. I was worried to death in the last few months of school because he was so unhappy. Now I'm worried about failing him. I don't think we will ever stop worrying LOL. A great big hug back to you and thank you." ~ Sharon

Will My Child Miss Out By Not Going To School?

❝ My fear about homeschool is that I will fail my child and myself. I am scared that I am not teaching him enough. I feel as though I am constantly forgetting a major concept or lesson, that I will prove all of the people who are doubting my ability to teach my child right." ~ Melissa

"I used to feel that my daughter was missing out by not being in school, but not any more. In public school my daughter was always behind. When it came to actual lessons, she either didn't remember, or she didn't want to talk about it. Now, she **lights up** when she learns something new and isn't shy about it. She knows if she needs help she can ask without feeling embarrassed. ..She was always scared to ask questions on any work at school because she feared being laughed at by the kids or getting in trouble by the teacher. Now she reads everyday, is already leaps and bounds beyond where she left off in public school last year, and everything else is better, including her attitude!!" ~ Cecily

"I used to feel like this in the beginning. Then I realized my son learns **above and beyond** what they reach in school. Thank God." ~ Saadiya

"Absolutely not. Hey your child will gain by not going to school. She/he will gain in **confidence**, self esteem and independence amongst many things. They will learn to view the world differently and will be able to discover and question things in a safe and non-judgemental setting. Your child will learn to set their on goals and have the full choice on what to explore based on their own natural fascinations ...The rewards are great for both parent and child...dive in!" ~ Katie

"I have always felt the biggest risk for my kids missing out on anything is their social life - especially having one with autism spectrum disorder. But I think it's a problem that can be addressed by making sure you fill any 'gaps' - join homeschool groups, sport teams, art classes, etc. My kid with ASD is now at our **local college** training to be a car mechanic so I feel it's worked well for us!" ~ Helen

"No, your child won't miss out because they will be able to develop at their **own pace**, be able to benefit from one-to-one attention, they will be able to develop a love of learning and have the freedom

to explore fully rather than be restricted by targets."
~ Lorraine

"Personally, I feel that my kids **get more** by not
being in a traditional school." ~ Bethany

"I have never and will never think this. School is
a pale imitation of what can be offered through
homeschooling." ~ Rich

"While I often find myself doubting my decision to
homeschool, I remember the public school report
card that showed an 'A' in performance with the
notation that she 'did not meet grade level
expectations.' While I was told this grading was to
help my child's self-esteem, no interventions were
offered to assist her. I realized she was just sitting
in a classroom and was being given the grades
necessary to pass her from grade to grade with
little concern as to how prepared she was to do so,
neither academically or socially, since she was
clearly not on the performance level expected." ~
Denise

"I think all of us probably have to deal with the
above question at some point in time, whether this
is because we ask ourselves this or whether other
people start throwing questions at us. But if we
think back for how long humans have been around
and compare that to how long a school system has
been in place, I find the question answers itself for
me!
    I am still finding that the so-called "socialization"
at school caused a lot of damage to my children.
Do I feel my children are really aware how
fortunate they are to be homeschooled? No. Do I
feel my kids sometimes feel they are missing out by

not being in school, because society makes them feel this way due to our choice to home educate? Yes. Does this make me feel like I am sitting between a rock and a hard place at times, because I know I am doing the **right thing** for my kids, but my kids and society don't see it? Yes. Will this change my opinion or my decision? No! **Trust** is the main thing here! Trust in my decision and trust in my kids!" ~ Simone

"There is a compromise to every choice. Schools have large budgets and can give access to opportunities that unfortunately are out of reach for some home educators. However, there is a balance...The **freedom** you get with homeschooling allows you to focus the education to allow your child to follow their passions, and experience life in ways that school education on mass would struggle to provide. Each family has to come to the decision themselves. For some, 'school' will work well for their children, maybe at different stages of their childhood or throughout. For others, homeschooling is a **natural path**, and most of us find ourselves on this path when 'school' hasn't worked for our children.

To those parents, I would say have the **courage** and faith in yourself that you can give your child what they need and there are so many avenues of opportunities and help to guide you with your journey. The anger and hurt you will feel at the failed schooling experience - try not to let it linger over everything otherwise you risk you and your child never moving on from that hurt. Embrace that life is a journey and that no one person has the 'right' path mapped out for them. There will be many bumps and falls along the way but life is not about avoiding those hurdles, it's about how we face them and who we become because of them." ~ Erika

"Each family is responsible for the education of their children. Education may be delegated to the school but it must never be abdicated. In truth, all parents homeschool. If a child attends school, parents see to it that children get to school. Parents oversee homework, work with school to ensure educational goals are met. Yes, children miss out by being homeschooled. And yes, children miss out by attending school. I am in awe of the parents who homeschool some and send some to school. That is a juggling act for sure! Dear ones, keep doing what you know is **best** for each of your children. I stand with each of you in your choice to educate as you see fit." ~ Traci

"I told my children about school in an honest fashion. My teens do not feel like they're missing out." ~ Jennifer

"I look at it the opposite way. My kids will miss out by **going** to school." ~ Corinne

Being Judged By Others

" **Ugh so today has been a power struggle. How do I get rid of the effect my own schooling has had on me so I don't inflict a school mindset on my daughter? The whole reason we homeschool is because school fails so many kids with autism and...they get bullied. I was feeling so discouraged this morning because you get judged so much if your child isn't doing things at certain ages."** ~ Kaitlin

And Helen has a similar problem:

"I'm having issues with family questioning my daughter and saying about school and telling her she **isn't learning enough**." ~ Helen

"The way in which we were educated does influence the way we do things but we must always remember that our **children's future** will be totally different from the world we grew up in. They will do what they need to do in their own time. I sometimes wonder who sets these 'milestones'." ~ Sheila

"My daughter has always done things in her own time and we try to respect that and not rush her. She was an early walker and talker but everything else she has been later and that's fine. That's her natural timing and as we homeschool that's fine. I want that pressure off so she can do things as she naturally gains interest." ~ Kaitlin

"I don't think there's any **magic pill** to take to rid you of the effect your own schooling has had on you unfortunately. So many homeschoolers have been to school, have family and friends who went to school, have often tried sending their own kids to school, watch kids go to school in movies and on television because really, that is the norm: most kids go to school. We know so much about school because we've had so much exposure to it and so many people telling us that's the only way to educate children.

As homeschoolers too, we might also feel we have something to prove to all the naysayers so we find ourselves pushing our children just to show them that our kids are doing just fine, - in fact as well as they would or even better than if they were in school (guilty!). I'm guilty of this because I'm sick to death of all the negativity about what I do and people frowning at me so naturally I want to just shut people up!

That's where **trusting** your child is so important. This hit home for me because I get frustrated with my son at times too. You really do have to trust your children, trust yourself, just do the best you can and then ultimately leave your children to be responsible for their own lives. Nobody, whether they went to school or not, turns out perfect. In fact, that's a pretty common saying: nobody's perfect. I think you have to focus on teaching your children what's important and that's a personal thing.

For me, I want my kids to think for themselves, be kind to others and I want them to learn how to learn. Those - along with basic reading, writing, math skills and general knowledge - I'd be happy. I'm sure you're doing a **wonderful** job - trust in that and enjoy your time with your daughter and enjoy her for who she is. She's her own person and when you get frustrated with her, maybe remember all the things you love about her and that make her special." ~ Ange

*"That TRUST your CHILD lesson is the hardest lesson in my free Courageous Homeschooling course. I began to realize the truth of it as I continued homeschooling and began to see that however much WE do as parents in the end it is up to your child. All you can do is **your best**. And reading this and the other posts on here it is so obvious that we are all doing our best - and doing it with love." ~ Sonya x*

"Sonya so true! We are all doing our best. You wouldn't put up with listening to all the rubbish you get for homeschooling if you weren't doing it because in your heart you thought it was **best** for your child. I know people who have been to very expensive private schools and had no interest in university and people who have come from tough backgrounds and with determination have built **fantastic lives** for themselves. People who have left school and pursued their passion even if that meant going against what their parents intended for them. I had one male friend who dropped out of engineering to become a ballet dancer and he loved it! It IS often up to the individual in the end to make what they will of their life. That's a powerful lesson for kids to learn." ~ Ange x

"For me, I've had to educate myself. I have had to challenge all the ideas about socialization, textbooks, my own agenda. I am constantly reading and learning about child and human development even with a master's in social work!! There is so much new research out on how humans learn and longevity, what brings **happiness**, what is the best way to learn certain subjects, etc. Also, I am always researching new curricula and some old ones. We love old Living Books and reading together.

This is a huge difference to how I grew up as my parents never read a single book to me. I went to school from 5am to 6pm - almost like a boarding school. And honestly, I learned very little and was petrified most of the time. But now, as an adult, I've learned a few things - had a few experiences and my daughter is the beneficiary to this. We visit lots of museums, and enjoy just fun times in nature. We do 'school' at home and enjoy that time also together. All of it feels very **precious**. My husband is around and he enjoys time with his daughter also. We are very close and know that our time together is limited, so we enjoy our very simple life." ~ Lely

"If it isn't working - change it up. Breathe. If you did do PS before make sure you and your child had time to deschool. They say three months for every year your kid was in PS. Find the innate love of learning. Which doesn't look like 'school' in any way, shape or form. Skip what is expected and **have fun**. Go to a museum (check - school for the day DONE!), hit the library (school done for the day!), go on a hike and use your body and your mind (school done for the day!).

Listen - it's all about the **joy of learning** for you and your kid. Find ways to learn at the grocery store. My kids have more social skills because they can hit the deli solo and order the cheese and have polite interactions with strangers. They are more confident and I don't have to wait in the deli line so WIN WIN! Play a game. Chess, Stratego, Tick Tack Toe, Legos, build with blocks. It doesn't matter the age. It's all logic based and its learning. Do Sudoku. It's math. Watch a cool movie. We read for fun and that was their only ELA for two years. READING. Breathe, have fun, find out what their passions are and run with it. You got this!" ~ Allie

"Every kid learns at their **own pace**. It is not a race. I have a child that didn't learn to read until he was 8 years old. I would get a lot of looks and comments because of it... Now, he is a fantastic reader and is doing awesome.

I do struggle with it sometimes. Are my kids behind? Will they ever get to where they need to be? I just have to **faith** in what we are doing and my kids prove to me time and time again that they are smart and right where they should be. I love those moments." ~ Ciarra

"MOST of the time, kids who learn at home are **ahead** of their public school counterparts. When my older one were briefly in public school and later college, they remained near the top of their classes." ~ Wanita

"One of the reasons I chose to homeschool my

children is that they will not be compared to other people, but will measure their own progress. Each child learns differently and has different **strengths**. I much prefer to build their personal strengths rather than worry what other people's children are doing."
~ Helen

"It's not a race! We have found our son learns things incredibly quickly, when he is ready and interested in something. On the other hand, if we try to teach something he's not ready for, or not interested in, it is a real struggle. The wonderful thing about home education is that we can follow his lead so learning is a joy. Watching him develop and learn is such a **privilege**." ~ Anna

"The most important part is: don't put too much pressure on yourself. You are and will be doing **great**." ~ Carina

I'm Not Good Enough To Teach My Child

❝ I think my biggest fears are all to do with not being good enough for my children - not patient enough, not energetic enough, not fun enough, etc. I so often find we don't have time to do everything and I shout too much and try to fit too much into the day.

My hope is that I can focus on the **good stuff** and find the fun again, start reintroducing the bits of the week that helped us all to feel good. We haven't done yoga since all being ill before Christmas so will try to get that going this week. And we can start to plan our new garden.

Any tips on stopping shouting that really work?" ~ Claire

"I share your fears... I worry that I do stress and rush around at times. I know I need to **slow down** sometimes..." ~ Sue

"If it helps Claire that fear of not being good enough is something I've heard a lot of homeschoolers say is their main worry. What I notice is that when someone ELSE is telling you that it's much easier to stand back and say: "Hey! Wait a minute - but she's doing really well!" I suppose this was what I meant about becoming your own **best friend**. It's a brilliant idea to start re-focusing on all the good stuff - and I love the idea of planning a new garden." ~ Sonya

*"Sonya, I know that talking more **kindly** to myself is the only place to start, I just find it so difficult to find ways to do that. I really want to feel that I'm giving my children what they deserve instead of a stressed, tired alternative!" ~ Claire*

"No answers, but lots of 'I hear you' and 'me too' over here!" ~ Katie

"I know unschooling is not for everyone, but I will say that becoming **delight led learners** eliminated the homeschool battles, especially with my creative visual learner. Now I facilitate their learning and support their interests. My goal now is to help mentor their gifts and talents. I think before, the yelling stemmed from trying to do school at home and complete all I thought I *had* to.

Unschooling takes a lot of trust, so I will not say it is easier, but I am thankful the battles are over and my yelling about homeschool is over. I am also thankful not to have a son screaming and crying about how bored he is and how much he hates school. Now he learns for the sake of learning and **enjoys** it. I realize that this type of learning won't suit every family. I frankly used to think it was a lame/lazy way to homeschool. I obviously feel different now LOL! Hope you find **what works** for your family." ~ Lisa

*"Thank you all for these helpful ideas, I've seen some of them before but stressful times often lead me to slip up! I should have mentioned that we are **unschooling**, we don't have any 'learning' battles, it's mainly routine things like getting dressed, getting out of the house in time for the various groups the children love etc." ~ Claire*

"Claire one thing that really helped us with the day- to-day stuff was 10 minute warnings! I realized my children made a fuss if I just went straight into wanting them to get dressed, leave the house etc. So I started telling them - "in ten minutes I need you to go get dressed because....." then "in five minutes I need you to go get dressed because" then they got a one minute warning and then I asked them to please go get dressed! Somehow this seemed to **soften the blow**! I think they mentally started to detach from whatever they were doing so they were happier to go and do what was needed instead. This worked REALLY well for leaving someone's house to come home." ~ Julie

"Ah, see, now I feel like there's something wrong with me or with my children. I've given them time warnings since they were tiny, 5mins, 10 mins, 1 min - we've tried everything but they just will not get ready or hear what I'm saying. This morning was typical. Opticians appointment, we have

to leave at ten. I got their clothes out with them last night (my son has OCD and won't get his own out) so they could put them on first thing. They didn't. We had breakfast, they had playtime, I explained we needed to leave the house in half an hour so it was time to get ready. They didn't. I got myself and the baby ready, gave them a fifteen minute warning. Nothing. Son playing drums, daughter arranging soft toys. Ten minute warning plus calm, gentle explanation that we really have to leave, can't go to optician in pajamas, need to brush teeth etc. but I really don't want to shout. Nothing. Five minute warning, gentle explanation that I'm now feeling really stressed but really don't want to shout. Repeat at three minutes to ten, really determined I'll stay calm. Both still lying on the floor, son now wearing pants but that's it, daughter still in pajamas. I start loading car, calling upstairs in case that encourages them. It doesn't. I shout. They finally come down five minutes after we're meant to leave, we're ten minutes late for the appointment and I feel like a horrible, crappy parent. They apologize and say it'll be different tomorrow. This happens every single day of my life." ~ Claire

"Gosh Claire far from you thinking you might be doing anything 'wrong' I think even a saint would have trouble with that one. Slightly stumped this end; you've done everything you could and of course there's nothing 'wrong' with your children either. I'm really not sure what to suggest - any ideas anyone? Except what I would say is that we all have 'bad' days/weeks and sometimes it's just a question of doing **the best you can** to weather through with as much patience as you can and finally things begin to change. Anyone else with wiser words to share?" ~ Sonya

"Ha! Don't worry Claire. We all have that at times too. Sometimes you just have to weather things and know that they will change in time. It isn't like they won't get themselves dressed when they are 18! Can they get ready themselves when it is something they want to do? Or do they never manage it? It is possible they are overwhelmed by the getting dressed thing and need more help/support. In which case you are just going to have to grit your teeth and be more hands on and practically do it for them until they are older.

If they can do it when they want to then I would use those times as an opportunity to praise them up. Tell them how **wonderful** they were to do it, how clever they are, what a difference it has made to the morning, how pleased you are and so on. Let them get the message that doing what you want them to is going to make them feel good and give them lots of positive attention. But most of all, don't feel like a crappy parent. You are doing a wonderful job. It isn't easy to be a parent (and it often sucks!). All we can do is the best we can." ~ Julie

"Yes, same here too! Now I'm not saying this is the case for you, but in my case there is definitely a bit of **modeling** going on - I may, just sometimes, get a bit distracted and think I've got time to just check Facebook and then end up later than I intended....Or I've said it's time to go but then I got involved in a conversation with someone....So I sort of can't blame them for doing the same (even though I do sometimes!).

Basically if we absolutely positively have to be somewhere on time (which thankfully isn't often thanks to homeschooling) then I try and leave lots and lots of extra time and to step in and actually help the five-year-old get into his ballet uniform and walk the older ones through toilet, getting changed, packing bags etc. But it still often ends up rather fraught and with us all running down the road dropping ballet shoes behind us. I guess it is difficult to be both laid back and flexible and at places on time - at least for me!" ~ Katie

"Yes, Katie, it's exactly that! No matter how much 'dawdling time' I build into the morning (or evening, it happens at bedtime too), we're always late. I know this needs to start with me making a change, I just feel frustrated that I've tried so many things and had no success whatsoever. I'm feeling much more positive about stopping shouting though - the last few days have been much calmer so perhaps if that continues to improve, it'll have a positive effect on co-operation too. Thank you again." ~ Claire

What If I Fail My Child?

There are two big concerns here – whether you are up to the job and whether you can really manage to teach your child enough to pass exams.

"Hi all I'm looking for some reassurance. I've been homeschooling for over 19 months now and although I myself see so much difference in my child I still find myself questioning my abilities. I worry if I am teaching her enough and I really worry I'm failing my child." ~ Helen

Helen says what many of us fear, and here's Sharon to share the other elephant in the room:

"I'm feeling overwhelmed and concerned that I'm going to fail my son. He's more of a outdoors farm boy and would far prefer to be out with his dad on the farm than any paper work. LOL. I think us moms worry more than the kids. I hear so many great things about home schooled kids. But am I the only one who's worried their child might not pass exams? Sorry to go on I just wondered if anyone else felt

like this and what's the best way forward." ~
Sharon

"My experience is that if you do something
different than most people you will get a lot of
reactions, a few positive, but mostly not. My humble
opinion is that even if they are not realizing it people
feel somehow criticized and offended, they realize
that there might be **more options** that the ones they
chose and they do not like it, so they will try to
undermine you to feel justified. I am sure you are
not judgemental, but they are somehow feeling
judged and they react. I think going against the flow
is never easy, but it can be extremely **rewarding**.
When I started to homeschool only my father fully
supported me (he said he knew it would work
because he had been homeschooled) and my
husband tried to do the best he could. After time,
many uneasy conversations and seeing how our
child is doing other members of the family think it
has been a good idea, or at least they **respect** us. I
hope that soon you start to get more support." ~
Maria

"I would love to give you a great big hug right
now. I think you are doing the **right thing** for your
daughter and you are doing a great job. I am
forever worrying, whether I am doing the right thing
for my kids. I will be the first to criticize myself, my
decisions, my actions and me in general and it leads
me to wonder, where this self-critical destruction
originates?
Personally, I think it is from growing up 'in the
system', going to school and having to follow the
general expectations! I sometimes wonder, where I
would be now, if I had had the time to think about

what I wanted to do in life, like my children can, if I had had **100% support** in my decisions and aspirations, even if they aren't the norm? I wanted to become a singer when I was younger. I tried as much as I could, contacting recording studios etc., but my Mom was against it and wanted me to go down the 'average' route of school and apprenticeship, which I did. I did temporarily get back into singing again in my early twenties, but the self doubt was already deep routed and planted, so I gave it up again, despite having many people around me saying I could make a career out of it.

What I am trying to say is, maybe you should try and look at your situation from a slightly different angle. Maybe, because you are allowing your daughter to **thrive** in homeschooling, she will never face the problems and worries you are facing right now. Maybe, if you had had the same chance when you were younger, things would have been different for you, too. So, really, you are not "leading her down the same path," so to speak. You are being more than **brave** and instead of holding her back, like so many of us have been when growing up, you are enabling her to spread her wings freely and learn to fly and to trust, that wherever her flight takes her, she will succeed. Sorry, I am being very philosophical this morning. I hope what I have written makes sense somehow. Big hugs." ~ Simone xxx

"Exams - my 3 kids just returned to public school. My oldest had to take the standardized test. He unschooled for the past 3+ years. He is 13 and is a Freshman in high school as of last Monday. He got a **perfect score** on the math test, and he got 95% for the remaining subjects. He hasn't taken a 'real test' since 3rd grade. So - please don't sweat it.

About your son liking being on the farm - that is AOK. Does he like to read? Can he read about how to farm better, or about agriculture - it really does NOT matter what he reads as long as he reads. 60 mins a day and he will learn to spell and write and do Language Arts because reading activates all those areas of the brain and if they can read and retain it then they can pass the darn exams...

Now math - Okay - so he's a farm boy - I'm sure you have to measure things (you can tell I am not a farmer LOL!) and you have to know things - like how much your cows produce - all math - etc. etc. Figure out what math he can learn and figure out how creatively you can get him to document that. Like your husband might want him to provide him with some statistics on X animal - that is MATH. Measurements - he has to measure fence posts I would imagine - so measuring is all of that too. Written work - honest to goodness have your husband join you and ask him to ask your son to write up a farm plan of some kind and that will be his writing.

There are creative ways to get it done without it feeling like "MOM I DONT WANT TO DO THAT!" Think outside the box - it's really what it is about. And math - well if it comes down to it - use Khan academy dot org - it's free and you do mastery challenge after master challenge but if you KNOW it they don't pester you with a bunch of practice questions. That is how my son got a perfect score on his math exams. HUGS - think of what will work for you. And he will be **successful**." ~ Allie

"I'm like you with the worrying. I've had a day like that today. It can be hard to think clearly and logically and **creatively** when we start to feel down about things. But Allie is right, there are so many ways to learn, and learn way better than in the classroom. **You can do this!**" ~ Brigid xxx

"The beauty of homeschooling is the **flexibility**. Remember, this is a marathon, not a sprint. Please be encouraged. Who taught your child almost everything he knows? YOU did! We all worry, no matter how we choose to educate. Most kids do just fine in whatever they choose to do in life. You got this! " ~ Traci

"You should have seen my first year homeschooling - first three months stunk like you wouldn't believe. I was crushed - I was sending them back - Why Oh Why did I do this? And then I began to let go and **trust**. They began to want to play chess and I was like "I'd rather poke my eyes out" and then we found NO STRESS CHESS - a game with card like instructions and POOF - we all played and they learned and I learned and we had FUN. They were giddy with ...well what else can we play? So we played - everything - and we went on field trips and we relished the museums to ourselves and then our family was like "WELL OH MY GOSH - how are they learning??? EGADS?!"
   SO - I said "Hey guys want to write a family newsletter each month? You can highlight all the fun we're having..." And then I had 3 littles - ages 6, 7, 9 - wanting to write up a newsletter but nobody knew how to type and that would be faster right?? They asked!?! So we found dance mat typing on BBC America and a month later they were all typing good enough to give the newsletter a try. So - the oldest and I formatted one - and they began to add their detail. Oldest was editor-in-chief, youngest

was an art and poem contributor and middle was the all around journalist. They each typed up a section. One wrote about monkeys - one wrote about...and so on and on.

They began to put this out once a month and nobody asked what we were up to any more - it was all detailed here and they learned to write but would still say: "HA HA we don't have to do school...HA HA!" And so on and so forth and they learned and I didn't hate it and they didn't hate me and it was well just amazing. SO **do what works for you** - it'll be OK." ~ Allie

"Wow. I'm guilty of the saying "You will have to go back to school I can't do it." Then I see his face and I'm heartbroken. But I feel everyone is waiting for me to fail. Thank you so much you've helped more than you know." ~ Sharon xx

"I've been homeschooling for several years now and I still have days when I say that! I think we all get wobbly moments from time to time. There are so many things in life that can make us feel under pressure or doubting ourselves. That's why this group is so helpful as the **amazing** parents on here share different ideas and perspectives, and caring support, and it puts us back on track." ~ Brigid

Homeschooling Fears

❝ So many fears. Will I fail my children? Will my daughter ever read well? Will they be accepted later in life? Will they be able to sit exams? Will they get into college, University if they wish? Will my son be able to cope in 'normal' life? Are my children missing out? Am I wasting my time? Should we be doing more? Is it Okay that they don't really want to socialise much?

I could go on and on, I worry lots. On good days I know it's all total nonsense and in reality I'd probably have the same worries if they were attending school. But at times these thoughts keep me up at night. Worrying I think is a way of assessing what I'm doing and making sure I am doing my best." ~ Ruth

"Had the same fears the first year and **understand** completely how you feel. My daughter was in school her first year and was constantly sick and developed a stomach ulcer. Paeditrician told us it is due to stress, a seven-year-old too stressed sounds a bit far fetched, but it was a hard reality.

She finished Grade One in school. My son on the other hand, they told us he was not ready for Grade One and we would have to hold him back a year. We got him tested and the lady told us he is more than ready. After this we started homeschooling. I saw a total change in my daughter from the first year; she was **happier** and more relaxed and after a few weeks at home her ulcer disappeared. My son reads better than other boys his age. With homeschooling we can shield our children from everything bad, from nasty, kids peer pressure, wrong influences and content not suitable for kids. We as parents can decide what we want our children to learn and they can decide for themselves what interests them. You as a Mom are doing the **greatest job** and remember a mother knows best."
~ Bianka

"I can honestly identify with all those fears you have listed. And I also think you have kind of answered this yourself already. You would have fears either way. I think the most important part is to try and make sure that the inner voice which knows you are doing the **right thing** and a very **good job** is louder than the voice which doubts what you are doing. I know it's easier said than done, but this is where we are fotunate with this group. If ever we feel the doubts are getting the upper hand, there is an army of lovely ladies (and a few gents too) to build you back up again and fight your corner with you. Remember, don't question your ability to teach your children, question the system that made you question yourself. Big hugs." ~ Simone x

"We've been homeschooling for about three years now and the doubts and questions still

*appear. I have to really hold on to how my kids were when in school and how they have changed. Soon after my children left, the school got a very bad report for poor standards so I'm sure I'd still be worrying if they were in school. I was worried enough to remove them after all. I was so **pleased** when I found this group as all the other groups seemed to be full of people who said they'd never looked back or had doubts and to me that just seemed mad. I felt so much better when I found I wasn't the only one having these feelings. I actually think I may have even given up and put them back in school."* ~ *Ruth*

"I think it's natural to worry but the quality time the kids get by homeschooling is far better than the time they would spend with a whole class of children trying to be taught together. And no bullying at home either. My daughter had below satisfactory attendance at school due to ill health. She hasn't been sick one day in the two years we've been homeschooling. **Health benefits** are a bonus too." ~ Sheila

"Absolutely agree. I too had phone calls hounding me because my son's attendance was so bad, because he kept getting ill catching things from others at school." ~ Simone x

"As I read through your posts, I don't see a bunch of fearful ladies, but a bunch of **loving ladies** who care a lot about their kids. It is heart warming to see the courage it took many of you to pull them out of school. I like how Simone printed her Courageous Homeschooling journal so she could grab it later if worries strike. That may be helpful for you too Ruth. Maybe a journal or a list of why you pulled them out followed by a list of the **wonderful changes** that occurred after you did. This would be a great thing to read when worries strike. Coming from a Christian background, I loved Sonya's Courageous Homeschooling e-course because it reminded me of things my upbeat Pastor says all the time about needing to focus on **positive thoughts** (scriptures) and things that encourage your faith and confidence.

He says we need to do this daily, which makes me think about this course and how these lovely **inspirational thoughts** and quotes need to become a part of our daily or weekly routine as well so they become the louder voice in your head than the doubting thoughts. Now isn't that wonderful?! I also like that Sonya has shared that Courageous Homeschooling is about doing things while you are afraid. This is what **courage** is. You are all very courageous already for doing what you have done just to get to this place! I am so thankful to have you all as friends!" ~ Lisa

Am I Doing Enough? Am I Doing It Right?

This is a question which comes up often so I thought we'd better get some answers!

"I too am thinking that this week but remember how valuable that **one-to-one tuition** is compared to hours sitting trying to learn with 29+ others. Must look at the bigger picture, and I was amazed at the weekend how far behind my daughter's friend's knowledge is and she goes to private school!" ~ Sheila

"No joke - when I first homeschooled the first 3 months we replicated the school day from circle time to gym time to end of the bell day - in 3 months they were crying - I was about to wring someone's neck and I called my teacher friend and she was like "Okay - where are they at?" (she worked at the school that they had gone to and I had worked there too.) I told her how far we'd gotten and she said: "ALLIE - GOOD LORD! **YOU'VE DONE THE WHOLE YEAR IN 3 MONTHS!**"

WHAT?? EGADS? HOW? Because the day is 45 minutes of math and we did that - but in school a 45 minute math class for 1-5th grade is 10 minutes of teaching and then do a worksheet and then pick your nose and go to the bathroom and do silent reading when you are done. So she told me to take the rest of the year off and we did and to go back the next year and MAX do 90 min a day - we never went back to any of it - we unschooled from then until now." ~ Allie

"Seems to be the week for self-reflection! I have had similar thoughts this week. Am I doing enough? Are they doing enough? I think we are doing enough 'extra-curricular' stuff but the academic stuff seems to happen as a side thing." ~ Diana

"My goodness you hit the nail on the head this week with your question! My son is just weeks away from finishing first grade and just now can read books intended for preschool age. But then I look back on the beginning of first grade where just opening a book made him cower in the corner. My in-laws, even my husband, think he should be doing work several years **in advance** because he acts and talks like a little old man, but he isn't. He is a kid and I wish the teachers hadn't pushed me and let me take my time to learn things." Angie

"The problem is nearly always what other people think. I have a 14-year-old who's a self taught hair stylist, has been asked to do hair for gym competitions, a pantomime, bridesmaids and offered an **apprenticeship** by a friend who saw her work on Facebook. Her formal schooling ended a few years ago and I did unschooling with her. Do I worry that we've done enough? Every day. She does too because her school friends are doing 12 GCSEs and she says how will I get into anything if I don't have them? Mad isn't it!!!!" ~ Hazel

"I think as homeschoolers the '*Am I doing enough?*' type doubts can really stem from the pressure we feel to 'prove' our decision to homeschool was the right one. We don't want to look stupid and we don't want our kids to look stupid. I have days when I feel we're not getting much 'academic' type stuff done and then I remind myself:

(1.) One-on-one tuition is so **effective**. The feedback a child gets when they're working is immediate. They don't have to guess or plod along, feeling scared to ask questions because they'll look stupid or, and unfortunately this happens, they'll get into trouble because the teacher is busy right now.

(2.) A child can learn **everything they need** to succeed in high school in 2-3 years.

(3.) My kids might not finish their reading lesson but when they ask a question, even if it is something that just pops into their head like, 'Mom, do all animals have noses?' (got that one today!), then we explore it. They're still learning, probably still reading while they're at it to find the answer!

(4.) Whether someone is homeschooled or goes to public school they can never know all there is to know. But we can all have unofficial PhDs in what we're interested in.

(5.) There is nothing like intrinsic **motivation**. When your child finds the thing that moves them they will pursue it. It's not something you can force. Kids should be allowed to explore whatever moves them. It's more important to teach them to love learning, to know how to learn and to have an open mindset. And I find when I remind myself of these things too I'm a better Mom and teacher because I'm more chilled and more able to connect with my kids and enjoy them during their childhood." ~ Ange xxx

"Can I just re-emphasize what Ange so rightly said: "A child can learn everything they need to succeed in high school in 2-3 years." My son William only really started academic formal work age 13. He took two exams a year. He is now at **Oxford University**. Did I worry if we were doing enough? YES. With hindsight, did I need to worry? NO." ~ Sonya xx

"That's awesome Sonya! That thought really does comfort me! And I just watched a Ted talk the other day by a homeschooling mum who unschooled her kids. Her son was obsessed with rollercoasters and just wanted to ride them all the time. Naturally she began to worry. Where is the love of rollercoasters going to get him, right? Well he became a paramedic. His Mom said she shouldn't have worried because her son knew who he was and he found the **perfect career** for himself!" ~ Ange

How Do I Tell My Partner?

It can be hard to get your partner on board. **What can you do to help?**

"To some people homeschooling is the dark unknown and that can be daunting and create panic. I **drip fed** my husband with the idea for about a year and then when he suggested it made it his idea!! LOL. I think if you have a very basic plan to show or give him it will help. Can you involve him? Can he do one or two subjects?? I would tell him that Sonya's son who was homeschooled has gone to Oxford University. There are lots of resources online and in shops so you can stay 'on track' if that comes up.

And do have **affirmations** available...I have tonnes of these on my mobile, they are great for confidence and answer just about any negativity you may encounter. If in doubt you can find out. Post on here, there's plenty of support in this group.

IF it helps I am a **qualified teacher** with over 10 years experience. I now run my own company. I put my daughter in school for three years and pulled her out for many many reasons. The education system is in a dark dark place at the moment and I am glad that we are out of it. School works for some people, not all. One shoe size doesn't fit all. Good luck."~ Sheila xx

Here's a reply from a **homeschool Dad** about what happened in their family:

"You say you are not courageous but scared, but don't forget that it is impossible to be courageous without fear. When my wife finally got the courage to mention homeschooling to me, I had already been **thinking about it myself**, so it is always worth discussing it. In the end it's about what's best for your kids and only you and your partner know what that is." ~ Joe

And what if your partner is anti-homeschooling? Allie has this advice:

"We struggled our first year too - in understanding how homeschooling works. **Deschooling** your families public school mindest is key - this is where your partner is coming from... It's not a judgement on you - it's more of a judgement on homeschooling in general and just not getting how real learning works. School is beating the individuality and the love for learning out of the kids. All kids must fit into the same square hole. If they do not they are squished until they fit.

You have to change the conversation at home. Don't report in how long you do work. Have dinner conversations about what you **learned** today. A nature hike can explore and you can learn - it doesn't have to be from a book and sitting down. Experiential learning can help your partner see how much your child is indeed learning. Play is the job of children - it is how they learn. Building kits - one can work for hours and learn how to engineer, problem solve, learn math skills.

My husband struggled for the first 2 years...- are they really learning enough? We are now in year five and they are on point if not beyond. When did my 8th grader learn to write a real essay/persuasive argument etc.? 30 days ago. Is that later than his peers in school? YES - but how long did it take him to learn how to do this - three weeks versus learning it from 4th grade forward. He didn't like to write - if I forced him - it was brutal for both of us. So I stopped.

My daughter loves art...How do we learn? - we do tons of art stuff - Does she draw for four to six hours a day or MORE? YES - and guess what - she reads about art, she watches YouTube about art, she emails her friends and relatives about her art. We use Khan Academy for math because I feel learning math is important and it works for us and the kids. They do 30 minutes a day and they are at or above grade level for math. Reading - they read voraciously. If your child reads daily - they are at or above grade level.

School kids schedules are so packed they are often not left the time just to read for fun. **Relax** - and just change the conversation. I did this in baby steps at our house. I would tell my husband - we went to the library today and learned about X. Math was fun today (it was baking for example - great way to learn fractions). We learned for five hours today (laundry, baking, hiking, reading etc.). It's all about how your partner sees learning and their personal experience. It's not reality for your child. But that's Okay. You are doing enough. It's all semantics and the language used. You both want what is best for your child - it's just being said differently. ROCK ON - YOU GOT THIS!" ~ Allie.

And here are some practical suggestions:

"Try and **sit down together** once the kids are in bed and tempers have simmered down and start talking it through. I am sure, once you help your husband to understand how homeschooling works and the benefits, etc. he will feel reassured and able to back you again. At the end of the day, you both want only the best for your child. You are doing great."~ Simone x

"Maybe there is something else going on with your husband, like perhaps he's fearful that if your daughter looks 'stupid' he will look stupid and who wants to look stupid? It's probably hard to say anything to your husband about these things without sounding aggressive perhaps. Maybe you can try writing him a **letter**? You could explain that you're hurt and how hard you work and point out the amazing things your child CAN do. I'm sure you've come too far to throw in the towel." ~ Ange

"Your husband needs to trust in you...I think you need to sit down with him and have a heart to heart about it if I'm honest. I would imagine it's been playing on his mind for a while and personally I think you need to sit down with him and find out what's really going on. **Believe** in yourself - you are doing a fab job as a mother and a homeschooler....He needs to wake up and see this." ~ Steph xx

"Not everyone understands everything at the same speed. It is stupid to compare them. Sometimes, I wish I could teleport over and slap some sense into people's spouses and family. It's like they think school is some magical place where everyone 'gets it' and suddenly understands and is on grade level." ~ Lisa

Will I Damage My Relationship With My Children?

❝ My fears are that we won't achieve the peaceful, loving and happy home environment that I am always striving towards; that my children will pick up more of my weaknesses and stresses than anything positive; and that homeschooling would somehow damage my relationship with them once they are adults." ~ Sarah

"Sarah - if it's any comfort - I think one of the overwhelming benefits of homeschooling is that you are much more **involved** in your kids lives which makes you much closer as a family. My son William is 16 and we have just reached the end of our homeschooling journey. He is now at college and I have been really struck by how my role has diminished into ironing shirts for school (we never did much ironing before!) and putting food on the table. I've no idea really what he's doing for the rest of the day. And he has no idea what Catherine my daughter and I are up to at home. He remarked on it actually and said how **cut off** he felt.

Meantime, my Mom taught me at home and she is now nearly 95. It's brought us much much closer and she has been really involved in my life all the way through, including helping me homeschool my two children. If you want to make a comparison, it's far more likely that the stresses and pressures school puts on children will cause arguments at home which will tend to divide you and push you apart." ~ Sonya

"Thank you Sonya - that's encouraging - I don't know why that is a worry because one of the reasons I wanted to home school was to have a closer relationship!! Perhaps it's an abiding fear I need to address because of my own experience with my parents (and I was schooled!!)" ~ Sarah

"I think as you say it's as much about **parenting** as it is about homeschooling - I have similar fears about not giving them the focused attention they would benefit from, passing on my bad habits, etc., etc. For me, it's not about whether school would be better - I'm pretty sure that it wouldn't - it's about whether *I'm* doing as well as I could/should/need to be." ~ Katie

"It's brought us all **closer** together as a family. When my oldest was in public school for kindergarten, she got to where she wouldn't talk much about school or friends or anything unless I asked and she'd answer with just a couple words.

She also had started to treat her younger sister differently.

After we began homeschooling, she finally told us that she had a couple kids in her school that bullied her. In kindergarten that could be as simple as name calling, but we all know it gets much worse sometimes. Now, we're all so close and my girls are the **best of friends**. They get to focus on their talents and interests as much as possible. They are safe, they aren't learning about unnecessary or awful things too soon in life, they're not being introduced to drugs and violence. Some may say they're sheltered and that's fine by me. They are taught about real life and we don't feel that they're too sheltered. They have time with friends and play sports in the community. And as long as homeschooling works for our family, we'll continue with this **amazing journey** that has helped our family grow stronger together." ~ Beth

"My daughter and I are **super close**. That doesn't mean that sometimes I don't get glares and a list of excuses when work is required." ~ Šárka

"I feel I am **closer** as a whole family. Better attitudes as well." ~ Mandy

"The first year was a struggle as we all adjusted but the siblings are closer than ever and we as a family are. It all changed when I had them lead. They took the helm of the boat and it's been **smooth sailing** ever since." ~ Allie

"The only time it ever had a bad effect was when

I felt the need to force my son to do schoolwork he did not want to do because of my preconceived ideas of what homeschool should look like and my trying to replicate public school at home, somewhat. It resulted in a lot of yelling and tears for both of us. When we became unschoolers and I embraced gentle parenting, everything changed for the better. It was just what we all needed.

There are these notions we have about what our little homeschool will look like. Real life will shatter these dreams, and often needs to, as they are unrealistic. Finding your child's **unique gifts** and intelligence and learning to let them direct their own path is really the key to their confidence, success and to a healthy relationship with them." ~ Lisa

How Do I Deal With Nosy Neighbors?

Sometimes it's not only the neighbors and the trip down the shops which is the worry. Could well be your relatives are the biggest problem because they just don't 'get' it - and also somehow relatives have a way of winding you up and making you think you're making a mess of things.

Here's a real-life example from Mandy:

"We went out to dinner with a distant relative passing through town. He started to ask my son what grade he was in...the normal drill. When he found out we homeschool he told my kids "Oh you'll be ruined!" Ugg." ~ Mandy

"You go with this for an answer and people will let it be..."Thanks...we are going to try this out. It's what we think is best for our family and for now this is our choice. Thank you for your support in this matter." If they pester you: "Like I said - this is our family choice. Thanks for your concern."

You got this - home education isn't like 'school' - it

113

is in no way shape or form like public school, or even private school. There is no way you can replicate school at home. You can't and that is why it's **awesome**. There is no round peg in a square hole problem. You can think outside the box. You can school outside the box. HECK you do not have to SCHOOL at all. You can frame it any way you see fit and the children will learn. They learn because they have freedom of movement and not time set to do XYZ. They learn because they can bond with you and learn with silly games and reading really cool books together. They learn when you bake and go visit your elderly neighbors and they become caring and amazing citizens because you can go explore your community during the day and meet all the cool people that live there. THEY SOCIALIZE this way. You can live at the library and museums if you choose. They learn there too.

It's all about what works for YOUR family. I bet nobody homeschools the same way and that is what makes home education **beautiful** because it is what works for YOU and what works for me might work for you but even so it'll look different at your house. Maybe you want to school at night - maybe that is when focus is best. Maybe its 7am or maybe it's noon or maybe you take a week off because you need a mental health break and that is AOK! Enjoy it - change it up if it's not working. Trust your child - trust in YOU. And perhaps to the friend who is close... "I really wanted to tell you but I was afraid. This is a whole new adventure for our family. I so want our kids to maintain their friendship and for us too. So let's be sure to carve out time together and thanks ahead of time for your support." HUGS - YOU GOT THIS!" ~ Allie

"I have to deal with this from certain folks in my family. I try to **stay away** from them. I come here to the group often to vent so I don't mind sharing the stage with you when you need to. We can't choose who we are related to and what others think of our choices, but there's no judgement in this group just love and acceptance, encouragement and understanding." ~ Angie

"I guess it is even more hurtful when it comes from family and relatives, as you would probably like to think there is more support from them. Unfortunately I have had to realize that most criticism towards homeschooling originates out of ignorance, fear and a severe lack of education of what education really means and unfortunately that does sometimes include family and friends....I sometimes wonder why they are so hostile towards our decision to homeschool or whether they are simply scared I have made a **better decision** about my kids' education than they made with my education.

Some days my answers are better, some days they are lacking a bit. How about you make some notes about what they might ask you and what you would like to answer them to it. I find once I have written something, it stays in my head better or you could even keep the notes, excuse yourself for a moment when confronted, check your notes and come back fully prepared with your answer. One big point is that I have started saying to people: Why do you question my children's education when we don't question YOUR children's education? Once everybody believed the earth was flat and anybody who suggested otherwise was seen as mad and evil. Just because the majority think they know about homeschooling, doesn't mean they do. I hope this makes sense LOL.

Anyway, sorry for drifting off. You have made the right decision for your kids and your life. As hard as it is, try not to let people and their uninformed opinions and comments affect you too much, you are doing a great job and you have our courageous family here, not related in blood, but in heart and soul, right behind you every step of the way. Hugs." ~ Simone xxx

"I hate those comments out of left field that you didn't see coming. It feels like they leave you doing damage control for your poor sweet kiddos. When we experience things like that, I just tell them that that poor person is clueless and simply a product of the public school system brainwashing. People like that can't think outside the box. I then remind my kids how **lucky** they are that they aren't so narrow minded and how they have unlimited possibilities because they can think for themselves and pursue excellence in what they love. Big hugs dear!" ~ Lisa

"Ask why they choose to send their kids to school, then say that decision feels right for them and you respect that. This is what feels **right** for you and they should respect your decision." ~ Emma xx

"The things that 'ruin' children are bullying and abuse - which they're much more likely to receive at school." ~ Brigid

"So many people rush to judge why we are

homeschooling. I just give them a lengthy and pedant explanation of how much my kids and others I know **benefit** from the individualized lessons. They don't ask me again." ~ Maria

"My home education officer told me my daughter was getting a **better quality** of education at home than if she was in school. I tell them that if I have to. Usually does it. I will not be beaten by someone I don't know being nosy." ~ Sheila

"I had the same issue AGAIN last week in the wine shop. When she asked, I rattled off the **grades** my girls were achieving and she soon shut up. People are so ignorant to what we do and see it as not 'properly educating' our children. Others are blown away when I tell them my girls are homeschooled. The girls kept our gardener busy for tweny minutes this week with facts about cats and dogs and my physio's assistant was so impressed about my daughter's knowledge on mammals she even gave her homework about the platypus. Onwards and upwards ladies." ~ Alison xxxxx

"If only the non believers would understand the benefits are far above public school. I get so nervous when my kids get grilled. We shouldn't but we do. Everytime my father-in-law sees the kids he says 'So what did you learn today?' Not: 'How are you?' This drives me crazy. I think he is trying to prove something. Thankfully, he accepts their generic answers. Hang in there and stay strong to your beliefs!" ~ Mandy

"Good day everyone went shopping this morning for supplies for our gerbils. We popped into the grocers on the way home, at the checkout the assistant said: Is it the holidays? I said no, she said: Are they sick? I said no, she then asks: Why aren't they in school?, I said they don't go to school they are home educated, she said: Is their teacher coming later? I said no, I am responsible for their education, she looked me up and down in disgust..... I paid for my shopping and told her to have a nice day.....The people behind me looked on in horror when she was questioning me. My daughters were very upset that I did not argue...but I refuse to argue with the stupid. I spoke to the manager who was horrified, she **apologized** and promised she would deal with this as we came for shopping - not advice or opinions! Happy girls again." ~ Susanne

"I really would want to shout at her. But you feel so much better not rising to these people. It's just such a shame there are people like this. But my motto is: **Don't rain on my parade**. Happy people don't judge; so these poor people must be unhappy." ~ Sharon

"Ah, that's not easy to deal with. Really feel for you. The only time we've been questioned, the poor checkout assistant burst into tears and said how she wished she'd known she could homeschool as her son had been so deeply unhappy at school. You never know what response you'll get, do you?!" ~ Jo

"I think you handled that really well. I also refuse to argue with stupid. That was a very classy way to handle that type of situation and a great life lesson for your girls." ~ Kaitlin

"I know exactly what you mean. My Mom doesn't understand how the kids can still be learning everyday, even if I don't sit them down with workbooks and worksheets. And then I get this look from her "Oh my goodness, she is destroying her kid's life with this idea she can homeschool them." I am fortunate that my husband is very supportive and has not the shadow of a doubt in what I am doing. I guess I also keep forgetting, that I am continuously **learning**, even about how to 'teach' my children or rather help them educate themselves. I can't believe how much I have learnt about myself since homeschooling the kids." ~ Simone

"I have a list of phrases in my head to deal with folks that question homeschool. The judgement and criticism can be stepped up a notch when your kid has a difference. I don't ever try to defend my choice or try to change anyone's mind. Their opinions are not my problem. Words and phrases I like that work for most anything someone says to you:
1. Uh-huh.
2. That's nice.
3. Ah.
4. You think....(repeat what they say; they can't respond with anything if you repeat what they say).
5. Mmmm." ~ Suzanne

"I say: "Thank you for your input. You may be right..." and walk away or just simply: "Ah - you may be right." Ending in that phrase is a known psychological technique called FOGGING - and it ENDS it right there. Are they right? HECK NO. But people who are jerks like to feel right so you let them and walk away." ~ Allie

"They have their negative opinions; it doesn't mean what you are doing is wrong. Everyone's education is slightly different but we all find a place in the world eventually. I have found family have stopped giving me their unwanted verdict about homeschooling since my daughter proved them all wrong by getting the **qualifications** she needed and then getting a good job. What to say to people is tricky, though; I don't feel any need to explain myself. I have taught myself so many things in life, from languages to practical skills. I know education comes from within first and foremost. The will to learn is what ensures success and as long as they're happy they will learn. Everyone knows this deep down; it is their anxieties that makes them negative." ~ Janet

"In the past my initial response to negative comments have always been defensive and snarky. BUT you don't win any friends that way. I've since discovered (and I read about this in a homeschooling book too) that often if you stay **calm** when asked about your decision to homeschool and you approach your response in a friendly way and are open to addressing particular concerns without any snark, it's weird but sometimes people actually appreciate it and settle down. This has actually worked for me.

I like the idea of sending your family an **email** before they arrive. Just be your beautiful best self and tell them that you know it's a topic that may come up on their visit and you really appreciate their concern for your kids. But then go on to tell them what you think they may be feeling, some common fears and myths about homeschooling. Then talk about how this is not the case with how you do things, and in fact those myths are not the case for many. There are so many resources/support groups etc. available to you and your children. Remind them that you are open to answering any of their questions. See what they come back with. It's maybe a way to start a dialogue and for them to gain an **understanding** of what you're doing and that's the thing about where all the criticism of homeschooling comes from: there is a lack of understanding.

So anyway, that's just a suggestion of how you might want to handle it. After that, if they were still unreasonable and causing you stress, well I'm afraid I'd just be getting my snark right back on and being somewhat aggressive back. If you are aggressive back and they know they can't bully you then they may stop. So I guess you just try the reasonable approach first and after you've genuinely tried that and found it's still not working then don't bother with reason because you are wasting your time. If people genuinely care and are concerned they want to understand. Anything else is coming from a place that is not your responsibility and you can't control. Hope this helps." ~ Ange xxx

"Why don't you get your husband to raise a **toast** early in the visit (even if it's only with a cup of tea!) to his wife and children and their efforts AND achievements since homeschooling. Cut them down in a nice way before they get a chance to nag at you." ~ Angie x

"I think often our first reaction as home educating families is to be on the defensive. If we can get that under control, I think that helps strengthen our stance. Years ago while my husband was deployed, some of his distant relatives took a cruise and stopped by for a short visit. They were both highly educated professors at the time, and my MIL was always pointing out how they were against homeschooling. I was sooooo nervous, and already very stressed. There had just been an earthquake near us that shook me up badly...

Anyway - all that was going on and I was scared they would be hit by a tsunami so I called their cruise ship to make sure they were Okay. I'm not sure if that helped soften them, but we had such a **lovely** visit. At lunch, they talked with my 3 older kids about math and science, and they were genuinely surprised at how well they understood things. I didn't feel like they were testing me, and I didn't get offended by advice they offered. My MIL still today tells me how surprised she was that they had only **positive things** to say about our kids learning at home. Maybe that story can help give someone a strategy for dealing with difficult people."
~ Jami

What Do I Do If My Child Won't Do Any School Work?

Motivating the kids is the BIGGEST secret to making a successful homeschool. That is why I have written a highly recommended book called **Homeschool Secrets of Success**: *How To Avoid The Battle Zone* so that we can share ideas and suggestions for what works best.

If you're thinking about starting homeschooling and wonder how you're going to cope, here's Elizabeth to ask for help. It's such a massive topic this only skims the surface so please do check out the *Secrets of Success* book which includes advice from a trained motivational counselor.

"Having a rough week. Both my girls are having trouble staying on task... My seven-year-old wants everything I teach to be fun, but I cannot make everything a game or exciting... My ten-year-old wants me to walk her through every math problem... even though she can FLY through her math solo if I bribe her (big mistake, wish I never used bribery)." ~ Elizabeth

"It may sound silly but I clap really loud when I see them drifting. Then as they look up I give a little nod as a reminder! Once they have almost come to the end of the task we talk about what they have learned so far. Then I tell them how **excited** I am to see the finished product. It seems to work for us. Try not to pull your hair out." ~ Claire

"One of the wonderful things about child led home education is there is no need to push your child to do things they don't want to do at the moment. I have also observed that there are times when it looks like they're not learning anything... Then all of a sudden they'll make a massive **leap** in something. I honestly think they need 'downtime' to allow their brain to reorder the connections and let things settle in. Sometimes it's just a day or two, sometimes a couple of weeks. I've learned to trust the process now." ~ Anna

"With us a **break** works wonders. When my kids hit 'gridlock', I have noticed the best thing I can do is knock it down a few gears, whether for a couple of days or a week or two. Hugs, I know it can be frustrating." ~ Simone

"We have always run a **commendation** system where commendations are awarded for good behavior in difficult situations and making breakthroughs with work. They are all written down and a trip or treat given every 10. I am going to have to start taking away commendations for negativity and rudeness, not had to yet, but the threat of taking one away has always been devastating for her. The commendation system does work well for us." ~ Sheila

"I'm happy to read this only because we struggle with the same thing. Knowing I'm not the only one helps. Yesterday we had to stop and walk away with my younger boy. **Fresh air** and a change of pace for 10 minutes did the trick. I was sure to tell him that we were going right back to work though. Sometimes what works one day might not the next. We are also working on a **reward** system. Each boy has a little chart that can earn a star. After 5 stars they earn a mom coupon that we wrote up together. Like free time on the iPad or movie time. The star means there was no crying, yelling, or negative behavior during school time. They also earn a sticker on each day of their calendar that they've done good work. The visual of what they earn or do not earn seems to help. Good luck!" ~ Jessica

"If I don't want to do any work then I take a **break** and do something else...Then when I'm ready I'll go back to it. I've learned there's no point forcing work, it just ends up rubbish and I put myself off even more. When I get back to it I often find I have a real **spurt** and soon make up the time I spent away from it. I treat my kids the same, though I still panic when it's not easy to see progress." ~ Ruth

"I used to fight those battles with my son. I was always having to redirect and scold. It was exhausting! My daughter on the other hand was a dream to homeschool and very cooperative. I think sometimes, it can be helpful to rethink how and why we are homeschooling. My son did not thrive in our 'school at home' classroom. I had to come to a realization that school methods of teaching and learning are often a very broken way of doing things. Rewards for learning devalue the reason we learn. Learning is its own reward. Kids naturally want to learn.

Out of necessity, I decided to unschool my children. While I miss the familiar trappings of desks and workbooks and crafts, or reading on the couch, my kids are **thriving**! They both know how to learn whatever they want and are regularly blowing me away with all they know. They understand everything from antiheroes and story arcs to how to program RPG maker on the 3DS. They know music styles and have taught themselves to draw. They know about world events and math concepts. They are both big readers and researchers. They are pursuing things that are important to them, writing stories, creating characters, etc...

Is it a bit scary for me not to be steering this ship? You bet! But my kids and I are **happy**. We don't argue over what they must be learning. My daughter even surprised me and has wanted to do more traditional high school lessons and is working on that at her own pace and I am assisting her as she needs me. I hope you find what works for you. Just know that your precious kiddos have a natural desire to learn, which is a key to success in a rapidly changing world." ~ Lisa

Socialization: What About Friends?

Socialization and worrying about whether your child will make friends if you choose to homeschool is one of your biggest fears when you think about starting homeschool.

It's also one of the things everyone else is most likely to bash you over the head about!

So what do other homeschoolers think?

"My five-year-old son just told me that he wanted to go back to public school because he missed his friends. No way that is happening but it kind of made my heart cry a bit. I promised him he would meet new friends.

My kids have acquaintances that we see through park days or field trips. I always make an effort to take them to events with other kids. Do your kids have friends?" ~ Mandy

"This is so hard. My three have said the same a number of times. I have six year old twin girls and a four-year-old and took them out of school five months ago. They seem happy day to day, and have active social lives with swimming, gymnastics etc. We see another homeschool family weekly and have dinner with friends twice a week. They still really miss seeing their own school friends daily though. I'm hoping with summer on the way they'll realize that spending the days doing lessons on the beach will make them see the **benefits** of homeschooling. I feel soooo guilty when they beg to go back. Good luck to you." ~ Cathy x

"I like the fact my children socialize with each other, can't say I socialized much with my family as a child. My kids will make friends but aren't in any rush to do so and seem to be more choosy since leaving school. My youngest who's never been to school certainly isn't unsociable either. It's the one thing I **don't worry** about." ~ Ruth

"Are there any other clubs your child could join? Such as Scouts, a dance class or similar? Our son enjoys his clubs and it allows him to have precious **playtime** away from us." ~ Janet xx

"Friends are more difficult depending on where you are. We did local area baseball leagues, library events (any and all) and local park days and homeschool groups and we only saw the people at the events. It just was the way it was but over time - we found friends through Scouts and other activities. Do yours have neighborhood friends? Cousins they can **skype** with?" ~ Allie

"Thanks all! I'm unsure about contacting any of the public school kids. Something in my gut is

telling me to stay away. I guess it's hard for the young one to realize they only 'played' with their public friends for twenty minutes a day. I think with time and continued outings hopefully they can make some buddies. We live in the boonies so no neighborhood kids here. I never thought of Skype, that is awesome!" ~ Mandy

"Mandy, I know what you mean about the gut feeling, I have been the same with the girls' old friends. They weren't real friends to be honest, so I always felt it safest to keep them at a distance since homeschooling. My kids aren't into any clubs etc., that is just the way they are, so we are probably quite reclusive.

I used to worry about it a lot, but now I just think to myself, they have **plenty of time** to make friends. I also like to use the example of imagining we lived on a very remote farm in the middle of nowhere, then they would just have each other to play together. Besides, I always keep an eye on how they interact with people when we are out and about or in my shop and they are very **sociable** around people of any age and if there are any other children in the park etc., they make 'friends' very quickly. I have stopped worrying over that. What is the point in trying to force something which will happen naturally eventually?

I have been trying to teach my daughter for years, that if you want to be happy in a relationship of any kind, including friends, you have to learn to be happy in your **own company**. Only if you truly love and accept yourself, you can truly love and accept somebody else. Hope this helps." ~ Simone

"Simone this is exactly what I needed to hear! My kids are the same when it comes to clubs, they don't want to join anything and I'm not going

*to force them. We are not church attendees and I don't feel right joining one just for the social aspect. After reading your response I can see they are quite social with all. This will have to be left to fate and I'm **Okay** with it!" ~ Mandy*

"There aren't meet ups or groups near me...I work with kids before and after school. I bring my daughter with me. She has made 24 new friends! (She's in gymnastics and karate too). She missed her old friends terribly at first and so did I. However I really don't now. They live close, so if they ever wanted to stop by they could. Again, I'm kinda glad a few don't. (Some of the children weren't very well behaved... Now I homeschool I've been very tough teaching my daughter about respect and earning anything you want.) We go everywhere. But.....it's fine right now just us doing these things alone. I'm **not worried** any longer about her having friends." ~ Nikki

*"This is a huge reminder to me Nikki. I totally forgot about the respect issue, this is where my gut feeling is from...Since we have started educating at home my son's character has been changed for the better. Imagine how fragile our little ones are and in school we are leaving eight hours of that development to strangers and other kids with questionable morals. I am so thankful for all your comments as it reminds me once again that I've made the **best decision** by bringing my kids home!!" ~ Mandy*

"My daughter would rather have real friends than fake ones. She calls school the place from hell and doesn't want to see anyone from there. She is very **content** in her homeschooling world." ~ Sheila

"I have no worries about socialization. I have no desire for my kids to act like other kids their age. In a multi-age environment the children actually learn from each other. The younger learns to help others and be responsible. The older remembers to be creative and **have fun**." ~ Bethany

"As long as we live within society there is going to be socialization. Children should learn to socialize with everybody, adults, children their own age, children of other ages, etc...I think this is actually **easier** with home schooled children...It seems that some people understand socialization as the interaction between people of the same age spending lots of hours doing the same, when in reality most of children in school do not know how to socialize with other people outside of their circle. Sad, really." ~ Celia

"I have not been in school myself for YEARS. I am still making friends. I have friends in my future I have not even met yet and I can't wait to meet them. It is the same with my kids. They keep making friends too as they **journey** along in life." ~ Karalu

"I've never worried about this. Between church youth group, our neighborhood, Boy Scouts, Girl Scouts, sports teams, and homeschool groups, we're more likely to have TOO MUCH socialization!" ~ Sharon

"It is one of the things I worry about, though logically I don't know why! On the one hand, while I had a fairly normal number of friends at school, if it weren't for Facebook I'd only be in touch with one - so it's not as if I'm depriving them of lifelong school friends! And, on the other hand, they do have **good friends** that they see regularly. But the nature of homeschool where we live is that those friends mostly live a long way away and it doesn't take much to disrupt contact, so it always feels a bit fragile. Interestingly, it's one of those things I worry about much more in relation to my girls (eight and seven) rather than the boys (five and two!). I think it's just that it's easier to tick boxes with school friends - you can invite the whole class to a party, go round to play for an hour after school and have social activities laid on.... whereas with homeschool it's all on you to organize." ~ Katie

"I may have worried about socialization before I fully understood homeschooling; probably because that's the fear everyone was always speaking to me about. My children make friends incredibly easily. When we go to the park, they instantly are friends with anyone who is there. They aren't afraid to speak to people of any age, which is incredibly **beautiful**. They make friends with everyone, young and old." ~ Ashley

*"You girls rock! I remember when I was twelve my Dad gave me a book titled 'How to be your own Best Friend' and I thought that was the funniest and most ridiculous book ever based on the title. I never picked up that book until my 30's and only then knew the **intent** of his gift." ~ Mandy*

Other People's Anxt. Over Socialization

So you're thinking of homeschooling and you know your child could well have a **better** opportunity to make **real friends** at home than if they were in school.

But how do you answer the nay-sayers? Here's some thoughts so you can hold your own and have the answers ready:

"When I first started out trying to figure out how to homeschool my eldest, everyone said the same thing: she wouldn't have friends or she'll have trouble socializing...I am personally an introvert and largely a loner since young until my adult years. I don't have friends by the hoards but **I do make friends**. And these friends I made aren't your Hi and Bye friends.

I went to national school, and it didn't help or

make a whole lot if difference to me that I attended school and was surrounded by so many other kids who just wanted to be popular or be in the in crowd... It was tiring...

I concluded going to school doesn't help one makes friends. Or to learn to socialize any better than a child who is homeschooled. After almost four years since the birth of my eldest, she has grown to be a very **sociable** young lady. Confident, loving and engages well in conversations with people from across all ages. Yes, ironically she's a total extrovert compared to my spouse and I. And it's fascinating how she is able to carry on a conversation with people of all ages.

Thanks Sonya for the **Courageous Homeschooling e-course** lesson on this topic. It encourages me and assured me that no matter what others say about socialization for homeschoolers it will all work out in the end. It's a Thursday here and these words of wisdom definitely made it a terrific one today." ~ Julyan

"So....All children who are publicly educated participate in extracurricular activities? All do sports? All have friends? Err...I don't think so. Smile sweetly and say that should your children want to do an activity you will provide the **opportunity**. We have youth group, community sports, friends and we homeschool. We are out and about regularly and interact with people of all ages. This is what socialization actually looks like. I have never since graduating high school only interacted with people my own age." ~ Traci

"Some village schools only used to have 3 or 4 pupils until they were closed down due to being too small. Was there a problem with socialization back then? Probably not!" ~ Joanne

"I don't want my kids learning the wrong things from kids their age. I rather them learn the **right** things from us. My kids are always around other kids (at the park, co-ops, homeschool skate, etc.) and adults so they can socialize with any age instead of just one age group." ~ Samantha

"My daughter could not find friends in school as she could not find someone with the same interests. She likes Japanese and the others thought she is weird." ~ Muraru

"The socialization stuff...My kids have so many flippin' friends that we run into everywhere we go, we always have a yard/house full of kids, we're always invited to stuff... It's exhausting LOL." ~ Bobbi

"I made friends for life as a homeschooled child and I'm sure they will too. However, I do want to be intentional about making sure that my homeschool children are familiar with what's going on in the **larger culture of childhood**. "Remember that movie, cartoon, toy, experience, etc.?" It's a huge point of connection in college and later on." ~ Elizabeth

"I've been getting a lot of 'you need to socialize your boys' from family. They socialize every weekend with friends and family... They are not and will not grow up to be weird little boys." ~ Jess

"We don't socialize!!! Uggg! My kids can talk to anyone from grown ups to babies, the homeless to millionaires. My kids socialize with **all kinds**." ~ Diana

"I don't have time in my schedule for my kids to be any more social." ~ Wendy

"I have to say...I'm still fairly new to homeschooling...but I've noticed there is most definitely a difference between public schooled kids and homeschool kids...in my area anyway. Kids in a public school tend to group together & pick on the weak/different or newbies. The homeschoolers seem to be more **open and accepting**." ~ Steph x

"My son's autism quirks can leave him prone to being picked on in social situations. I can't shelter him completely from this but if I sent him to public school it would be like throwing a sheep in with the wolves!" ~ Kristina

"What makes people think that public school is the only place for a child to learn social skills, or that it's the best place for it? I do not want my children shaped by that environment. I'm raising strong, independent, creative individuals with healthy self esteem and good morals. They have wonderful social skills, too. They're **friendly and warm**, and can hold mature intelligent conversations with anyone. A confidence I believe that has been fostered by being schooled at home, where no one tells them they aren't good enough because of how they look, or dress, or makes fun of them because they're different." ~ Jennifer

CONCLUSION

Sonya Chappell

Things I Am Grateful For

"I am grateful for the opportunity to homeschool our girls - to have them **raring to go** every day as soon as they get up is such a gift.

Their confidence this week in particular has amazed me. My littlest T decided this was the week she was going to overcome her fear of putting her face and head under the water in her swimming lesson - such a massive milestone. And my little A who is always willing to give everything a try - so not like me at all! I'm grateful to have such a wonderful and supportive husband. None of this would be possible without him. And last but no means least, I'm grateful for the support of this group and all you lovelies who are all amazing. Thank you for sharing your journeys and for making me realize that wobbly days are still **Okay** no matter how long you have been doing this." ~ Samie xxx

"Just now, I was thinking how grateful I am for **online shopping**! A bundle of bags delivered to my door saving me a half day out of the week hauling all four children round a supermarket... Little things! I'm thinking of ordering some chocolates in next week's shop to pass back to the delivery driver to say thank you." ~ Katie

"Today I am thankful for having this opportunity to home educate my daughter, where she can drive her own learning, where we can go at our **own pace** and take a break when we want to." ~ Sheila

"I am grateful for the **freedom** I have in homeschooling. Our education can be tailored to the student instead of the student for the education." ~ Traci

"I am grateful for our garden with all the lovely produce ripening at the moment. I love harvesting!" ~ Diana xx

"This week I'm grateful for all the **extra cuddles** I get from both my boys as we learn together. And I'm grateful for having the time to go book shopping with my son for books on subjects he is interested in (books on Mars this week!), and not books he has to read. And I'm grateful for being able to round off the week with a trip to a café to enjoy **chocolate cake** with both of them." ~ Ange

"My daughter is starting to read, joyfully and in her own time!" ~ Dawn

"Today I am grateful for having a roof over our heads, food in the cupboard and clothes for us all to wear." ~ Catherine

"Today, as in everyday, I am thankful to have two **beautiful girls** that are well mannered, excellent students and that love each other dearly. I'm also thankful for my wonderful husband who has supported me for many years through the ups and downs and finally, this lovely group for allowing me to share my daily goings on and for allowing me to see what wonderful things you all get up to with homeschooling." ~ Alison xxxx

"I'm over the moon thankful for this group. God has sent so many wonderful **positive people** my way through here." ~ Nikki

"I am thankful for how the kids have **worked together** this week, supporting each other and taking control of the task. I am very thankful for a roof over our head, food on the table and the company of my lovely family. I am also very grateful for being part of this group. Only through this group do I now have confidence in homeschooling my children." ~ Simone xxxxx

"I am thankful as ever for the **amazing support** this group gives and that I was able to show to the education authorities why homeschooling is vital to my son's health and happiness and to be told he never has to return to a mainstream school." ~ Lorraine

"I'm thankful for my family and the **privilege** to have my kids stay home to learn." ~ Jami

Sonya Chappell

An Inspirational Homeschool Mom's Story

Let's end with my friend Rachel who homeschools her eleven children. Sharing homeschooling experiences can make all the difference. What a comfort to find that many of the problems we face are the same but in the end it's all **worth it**.

Rachel's Story:

Nine years ago, my husband and I took our children out of school to begin homeschooling them. We had six of them at the time, which seemed like a big family to us!

Full of **enthusiasm**, I read everything I could lay my hands on. I spent crazy amounts of money on workbooks with gold, shiny stars in them. I made beautiful timetables for each child on different colored paper, with boxes to tick, lists to check off and elaborate filing systems to store them under.

My children were going to be well versed in the classics, in history and in 'good' literature. We were all going to get up with the sun and devour math for the **sheer love** of it. The children were going to spend their afternoons building dams across streams, creating wormeries and digging joyfully on the allotment, wondering at the beauty of nature, free spirited and filled with peace and harmony. It was going to be a lot like *The Famous Five*, but more educational.

Alas, it turned out that I didn't have an Enid Blyton style child among them. What I actually had was a child who wanted to sit in his room all day and read about particle physics and computer programing. Yawn. I had a child who would dutifully plough through every workbook I gave her but never really enjoy it. I had a child who wanted only to do the exact opposite of anything I suggested. I had a child who wanted to paint, and paint, and paint.....and nothing else. I had little ones whose great joy was to find ways to disrupt everyone else. My filing system descended into chaos.

Over the years, four more children arrived and with each pregnancy and new baby, I would look around me through the fog of exhaustion and despair over days of having nothing to report, no 'enriching' books having been read, no foreign languages learned, no studious activity round the kitchen table. I spent my days veering between coaxing and threatening my children to produce something – anything – on paper so that I could tell myself I was doing a **good job** and they were learning.

Fast forward to today, and we have an oldest child who has completed **college** and is about to leave home to start his career. We have another child who is about to start her high school diploma. We have 3 more children who are all at various stages of **courses**, with several exams taken and passed. We have younger children who all have busy and interesting lives, packed with all sorts of schemes, intrigues and passions. We have toddlers and a baby on the way.

So what were we actually doing all those years and how did any of our children end up literate? I insisted that they all did some math every day because I believe that math is incremental and I didn't trust that a scattergun approach would work. We used Story of the World, a history and geography program that worked with all ages and abilities. We didn't use it every day, or every week, but we gradually covered a lot of history. We put a very high value on learning to read, and provided lots and lots of books via the library and thrift stores.

We did lots of reading aloud. We went out on trips and walks, tried out **new experiences** whenever we could and did a lot of chatting. We cooked and played and got on with our lives. Most important of all, we took time to sit down with each of the children as individuals, to discover what **their interests** were and what they wanted to learn.

It finally dawned on us that there was no point expecting our computer geek oldest to come and spot bats with us, or ask our would-be social worker to make a clay sculpture. Our children wanted to learn about archeology, equal rights, horse riding, rocks.... They wanted to learn what they wanted and our job was to point them in the right direction, provide what they needed and **encourage** them all the way.

As they got older and began to look at potential careers, our job remained the same. We helped them to research the qualifications they would need to get where they wanted to go, and then we **facilitated** the courses and the exams.

When I look back to the early days I realize that I was guilty of projecting my rosy view of homeschool on to my children. I had a beautiful vision in my head of a lifestyle in which I was a smiling, patient Mom to a super intelligent brood of high achievers who would dazzle us with their emotional maturity and broad general knowledge. I had visions of freshly baked bread straight from the oven, served up in a studious atmosphere.

Thank goodness our children were a lot wiser than I was. They taught me that homeshool is an extension of family life and happens amidst chaos as well as calm. They taught me it is all about individuals, all about coming alongside our children and encouraging them to develop into the best people they can be, whether we have eleven children or whether we have one, and I will always be **grateful** that we took the journey together.

More Help

Starting homeschooling can feel very lonely and isolating as an adult, especially as you feel the eyes of the world are upon you.

I hope this first of three Courageous Homeschooling Handbooks helps you discover the **delight** of homeschooling and answers the questions, insecurities and doubts we all face at the nerve wracking start of your journey.

You will benefit tremendously from seeing how others have found their path through decisions over how to teach their child best, which curriculum (if any!) to use, and real-life solutions to how to help teach different subjects. You will find the answers in **Parts Two** and **Three** of the next two **Courageous Homeschooling Handbooks**.

Together they form a **complete guide** to the most common issues that all homeschoolers face so that you can create a happy and fulfilling life for all of you.

One of the biggest keys to success is getting the whole family on-side, engaged and in love with learning. My highly recommended book **Homeschool Secrets of Success: How to avoid the battle zone** tackles this fundamental problem and unlocks the biggest key to homeschooling success.

"Read it and loved it. This is a superb book which presents a clear guide on how to build a wonderful homeschool." ~ Amazon 5 star review

My website at *www.homeschool-activities.com* is the place to go to find free resources, curriculum advice, fun learning activities for all the key subjects like Science, Math and English, art and craft ideas, and general help and advice on all aspects of homeschool.

You can also subscribe to the free *Monthly Activities newsletter*, which is full of activities for **all ages** based around fascinating themes like Art, Science, Math and Crafts. You'll also find lots of freebies, interesting websites, recommended books, even recipes and gifts!

Finally, I know that you will have your own individual questions, concerns and worries. You are very welcome to come and join us in the **Courageous Homeschooling Facebook Group**. All members are dedicated to helping and supporting each other through the ups and downs of homeschooling however you choose to homeschool. I'll let some of the members speak for themselves:

"I am very grateful for being part of this group. Only through this group do I now have confidence in home educating my children." ~ Simone xxxx

"Today I wanted to say that I'm grateful for this group, which has not only given me the confidence to accept that we are doing the right thing but also for the many friends I have made both near and far." ~ Sylvia

"I really appreciate having the space to be honest about how things are. This is such a supportive group. Everyone has made me feel so much better and stronger this morning." ~ Penny x

"I am enjoying this group so much. Its members are from all over the world and they each homeschool in their own unique way. Each however is committed to doing the best for their students. Hope you enjoy it as much as I do!" ~ Traci

My thanks go once again to all those from the Courageous Homeschooling Facebook Group for opening up the real world and dilemmas which face all of us when we choose to homeschool.

I trust that their words will bring you **strength** and **comfort** and help reaffirm your resolve that teaching your child at home is the best decision you ever made.

Thank you for reading! I do hope you found this book useful.

And I wish you much joy on your homeschooling journey.

Best wishes

Sonya

PS If you enjoyed this book, it would be great if you would tell your friends, your homeschool group and post a short review on Amazon.